A BONK ON THE HEAD

BY JACK POPJES

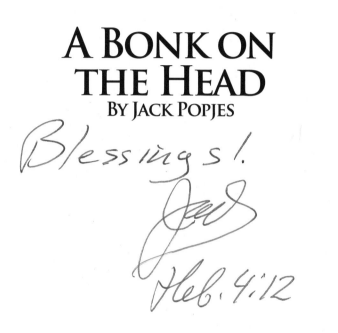

Blessings!

Feb. 4:12

Wycliffe

Partners in Bible Translation

Orlando, Florida
1 800 WYCLIFFE • www.wycliffe.org

Visit Wycliffe's website at **www.wycliffe.org**

To order additional copies of *A Bonk on the Head*, contact Wycliffe's Media Resource Center, 1-800-992-5433, *mrco@wycliffe.org*

11   12   13   14   15   16   6   5   4   3   2   1

CONTENTS

Foreword

Thousands of people have heard Jack Popjes because of his public speaking ministry. Many more thousands know him as an author, having read his weekly columns, his blog, or his books. I learned to know him long before he published his first book.

I first met Jack at an international conference of Wycliffe home organizations and their field partner organizations. I thought he was just another North American or European man in a leadership position. But I changed my opinion the first time he opened his mouth on the subject of Bible translation.

Jack was different—he didn't argue his points. Instead, he told stories drawn from his decades of personal hands-on translation experience in Brazil. He told them with passion and conviction, letting the stories themselves make his point. He obviously had a heart for pioneer missions. He was also a fountain of creative ideas to move Bible translation ahead. What startled me into paying even closer attention to him was his enthusiasm for fully involving nationals in Bible translation in their own countries.

Jack's vision of the future of worldwide Bible translation had nationals organizing and operating a Bible translation organization fully staffed by nationals. He did not see nationals simply as co-workers with expatriate translators. He saw them in charge of the translation program. He cast vision for interdependence between national and foreign mission organizations. As a citizen of Papua New Guinea, and the director of the newly formed Bible Translation Association of Papua New Guinea, that excited me.

I met Jack again some years later, when as Executive Director of Wycliffe Canada, he visited my country. He again encouraged me and the other members of the Bible Translation Association by asking perceptive, deeply penetrating questions. At the end of his visit, he told me he recognized that our group of nationals needed expert training, and top level consultants to help check our work, as well as project funding from outside the country. As the leader of a major Wycliffe organization, he did what he could to meet our needs.

For the past six years, Jack has been the featured speaker at Bible translation promotion banquets put on by Wycliffe Associates in the U.S. He often speaks in fifty different cities each year. I assumed he would speak passionately about Bible translation. But I was delighted to hear some of these banquets had been raising significant funds to help national translation projects in the island of New Ireland, off the east coast of Papua New Guinea. Go Jack!

I have responded numerous times to Jack's weekly e-mail columns thanking him for sharing his stories so filled with wisdom, insight, and often humour. They always leave me thoughtful, inspired, and encouraged. Since some of his columns are included in this book, I'll quote some of my immediate responses:

Power of prayer. "Such powerful truth and wonderful testimony. I'm forwarding it to all my staff, my board members and field workers."

God using elderly people. "Thank you very much for stirring my heart and spirit with these stories. I'm so excited to read about what God can do through elderly people."

A survey on the effect of being generous. "This is such an essential topic. Thank you for sharing these findings."

A recruitment event where young people go through a strenuous weekend. "What an exciting way of involving people in this great task! This got me thinking further about the possibilities of getting young Papua New Guineans involved in Bible translation, especially focusing on specific translation projects. I'd be interested to talk with you further about this to learn from your experience."

Personal questions for accountability. "Jack, this is very helpful to me. It's great to have your specific questions to help me frame mine better. I will send a copy of this to my senior administrative staff."

Cultural and biblical ways of handling conflict. "Thanks so much, Jack, for this wonderful epistle. It's a powerful reflection and revelation of what we experience all the time. Our PNG (Papua New Guinea) culture handles conflict in the same way as the Canelas. It's so subtle. I appreciate your thoughtful message. I've taken it to heart."

A vivid paraphrase of Matthew 25:31-46. "This is fantastic! Thank you for such insightful thoughts. Sorry we can't talk more face to face.

We in Papua New Guinea have generations of experience in storytelling. My friend and colleague Jack Popjes would fit right in around our campfires. His stories fascinate and leave his readers thinking differently. I heartily recommend this book.

Read it, enjoy it, but be warned, these columns will make an impact on you.

David Gela
Executive Director
Bible Translation Association of Papua New Guinea

Author's Preface

This book started sixty years ago when a crumpled piece of handwritten paper fluttered out from under my cot as I swept the old farmhouse attic bedroom.

I picked up the bit of rubbish left by a previous tenant, smoothed out the wrinkles, and tried to read it. That was not easy. My family had arrived as immigrants from the Netherlands only four months before, and I was still learning my first few hundred words of English. I noticed that it had been written by a grade seven student—someone my age. Then I deciphered her topic, "Why We Have Fingernails."

I was astounded! I had never considered this topic. Fingernails? They just were. Period. What's to write about? She, however, waxed lyrical about how useful fingernails were: for scratching yourself when you itch, picking up small things, increasing finger sensitivity, protecting the end of the fingers, etc. I was amazed! How did she think of those things? Where did she get those ideas? I know *I* certainly had never had a lesson on "The Usefulness of Fingernails."

My six years of education in the Netherlands had mostly been rote memorization of facts—something I hated and failed to do well. The writing class focused exclusively on calligraphy: making words and sentences look good on the page, with no thought of the content or ideas expressed. It was all about hand-eye coordination and nothing about developing thinking ability. I couldn't make those letters and words come out neatly—I still can't—but I loved to read books and make up stories of my own.

The rest of that morning, as I hauled water from the pump in the yard and chopped wood for the stove, I kept wondering: Someday, would I be able to think deeply about subjects I had never thought about and then write down my thoughts in an interesting way? The Great Author put that idea into my mind to incubate.

I loved to tell stories and jokes to my friends in Holland. Now in Canada, I was deeply frustrated at not being able to understand my friends' stories, let alone tell them my own. I was driven to learn English—fast.

Years later, I found an outlet for my writing skills and love of storytelling when I became a young pastor. Then, during the decades my wife, Jo, and I worked as para-linguists and Bible translators in Brazil, I practiced my skills increasingly as a furlough speaker and letter-writer.

The Great Author used a grade seven essayist to get me started, but that was just the beginning.

During our life in Brazil, one of the jobs I most hated doing was processing my monthly ministry receipts. The Brazilian tax authorities required us to copy all the receipts neatly in triplicate, with the exact code numbers, dates, and amounts filled in the proper columns, before we could use them as monthly income tax deductions. No errors, cross outs, or erasures permitted! Aaargh!

This loathsome task forced me to operate right in the middle of some of my worst weaknesses: arithmetic, neat writing, exact details, accuracy with numbers, and mind-numbing repetition. A morning spent in this drudgery ruined me for the entire day. Moreover, I did not suffer in silence! My wife will bear witness.

One morning, I slouched my way into the mission centre finance office, a folder of receipts in my hand, slumped down at a desk, and began the loathsome chore. The bookkeeper, noticing my obvious distress, took pity on me and made me an offer I could not refuse.

"Jack", she said. "Our family is due to go on furlough in fifteen months, and we need some new, up-to-date stories for our talks in churches. If you will write out a story of your experiences among the Canela and bring it with your monthly ministry receipts, I will process them for you."

Yippee! I jumped up, ran home, sat down at my typewriter, and wrote not one, but two stories. I ran back to the bookkeeper's office, handed her my receipt file and the two stories. She was delighted. I was delirious with joy to be freed of that odious task, and I floated home with my feet three inches above the sidewalk. By the start of her furlough, she had a collection of thirty exciting and inspiring stories, and I had a thick folder of professionally filled in income tax reports. Even more important, I had begun what is now a file of hundreds of anecdotes, stories, and illustrations.

> The twelve-year-old boy who wanted to think original thoughts grew up to write those thoughts, illustrated by his personal experiences. His writing led to the columns that make up this book.

> Read about a man who prayed for sixty-two years before he received the answer.

> Our God is business-like. How much market share does He want, anyway?

> All major world religions have preserved the words of their founders in the very language in which those founders spoke them. Not Christianity. It is unique. What are the implications?

> Matthew, Mark, and Luke quote Jesus using the term "repent" only six times, but the term "Kingdom of God" seventy-seven times? Here is why.

> A missionary jungle pilot laid the groundwork of faith among the Canelas ten minutes before he landed his plane in the village for the first time. Here's how he did it.

> Most grandkids think their grandmothers are close to perfection. Mine was not!

> Why are elderly Christians an army that Satan hates?

> Who can do Bible translation better and faster than a North American, seminary-trained linguist/translator?

I thank God for the many people He led to give input into these pieces. At least twelve hundred readers responded via email to these columns: some with encouragement, and others with perceptive comments, corrections, or suggestions for improvement. God gave my wife, Jo, discernment in many areas and the ability to critique my first drafts of the Canela Bible translation. She now comments on everything I write. A colleague from Brazil, Jim Kakumasu, also read each column and remarked on many. My daughter, Leanne, brought a fresh pair of eyes that resulted in penetrating questions such as,

"Huh?" as well as brilliant insights and advice such as, "Dad, you have two conclusions. Pick one!"

Special thanks are due to Dr. Natasha Duquette, Associate Professor in the Biola University English Department, Los Angeles County, California. She offered three of her former students—Biola English Department senior Turell L. Peshek, and graduates Tiffany E. Burish and Steven Vander Wall—the opportunity to edit the book. They went through the manuscript word for word, correcting everything from spelling and awkward constructions, to the formatting of the footnotes.

Thanks too, go to Kristie Frieze, Wycliffe's Director of Integrated Marketing Communications, to Angela Nelson who made further editorial suggestions, and to Dustin Moody, publishing coordinator, who shepherded the publishing process.

A BONK ON THE HEAD

It happened too fast to fully understand. My reaction was instinctive, instantaneous—and it saved my life.

For several months during the year between completing high school and starting Bible school, I labored as a pick and shovel man. I dug up water and sewage lines, except on those days when I "lucked out" with a plugged sewage line. Then I left my shovel on the truck, donned a pair of rubber boots, set up a barricade in the middle of the street, and pried the cover off a sewage manhole with my pick. Next I had the privilege of clambering down into its odiferous depths to clear the pipes of material that should never have been flushed down a toilet.

It was almost quitting time that fateful day when I finally cleared up the stinking mess and my partner let down the end of a firefighter's hose. I flushed the pipes, making sure everything was moving readily downstream, then sprayed some water on my boots to rid them of at least some of the stench, and hollered up to my partner to shut off the water.

I climbed up the steel U-shaped rungs set into the concrete and poked my head out of the manhole in the middle of a city street. Thankfully taking a deep breath of fresh air, I squinted as the sunlight glared off a massive chrome bumper on a car speeding towards me.

Another punk, I thought, *just trying to scare me again.* As I climbed up another step, I suddenly realized this car was coming too fast. It was way too close to swerve aside. The left front wheel was heading directly for me!

I reacted instinctively, let go of the rungs, and dropped. I heard a crash, felt a bonk on my head, and landed awkwardly on the wet floor of the manhole ten feet below. I groped for my aluminum hard hat and examined it, half expecting to see a dent or the black mark of a tire tread.

I climbed painfully back up and cautiously stuck my head out again. There was nothing to see, no barricade, no tools, no pails. I turned the other way and saw a car slewed sideways in the road, the driver shakily climbing out, staring at me white-faced and open-mouthed. Splintered barricades, dented pails, and miscellaneous tools were scattered everywhere.

As I climbed out of the manhole, the driver rushed up to me shouting, "You're not dead? I thought I had killed you! I was blinded by the sun when suddenly, there was this head! Right in the road! I felt this crashing bump and thought for sure I had killed you."

My partner ran up to us spouting more information. "I looked up when I heard a car coming! All I saw was your head right in front of his wheel! Then the crash and stuff went flying everywhere. I was too scared to look down the manhole. I expected to see blood and a headless corpse."

A decapitated cadaver is exactly what he would have seen if I had stuck my head out a few seconds later. And something worse if I had come out a few seconds earlier and been half way out of the hole and too far to drop back down to safety. I got a bonk on the head in only a split second, but the lesson learned stayed with me for life. Someone out there wants me dead, but Someone Else wants me alive—and He is ultimately in control.

After the manhole incident, I remember asking myself, "What does God want me to do with my life? What did He preserve me for?" For starters, I confirmed my decision to go to Bible school. That began a chain reaction of other choices and decisions: marriage, pastoral ministry, then the move to Brazil culminating in the completion of a Bible translation project for the Canela people, followed by a missions leadership ministry, and now service as a public speaker, writer, and author.

I took the bonk on the head as proof that God had something major for me to do. He did. And He reconfirmed that fact periodically throughout my life. I can list at least eight other occasions when, not through my own carelessness or fault, I was in extreme danger, but escaped death. Each time it happens I remember what David Livingstone wrote: "I am immortal till my work is accomplished."* I take each escape as God saying, "Jack, I still have something for you to do."

Let's see, the last narrow escape was just before I published my first book. The third book is coming out this year. Hmm? . . . What next?

Isn't serving God exciting?

*Eugene Myers Harrison, "David Livingstone: The Pathfinder of Africa," Wholesome Words, http://www.wholesomewords.org/missions/giants/biolivingstone.html

THE BELFAST LETTER

The translation teams at the conference in Brazil envied Jo and me. When we got together for problem solving sessions, fuelled by Brazilian *cafezinhos*—those tiny cups of strong, well-sugared espresso—Jo and I just could not identify with the problems they were sharing with us.

"We are ignored in our village," one team would say, "please pray for us." Another would report, "No one in our village will help us learn the language." Another from a different language group would chime in, "No one is interested in learning to read." Someone else would ask, "How can you get good storytellers to help you translate the Bible?"

We prayed for our colleagues, but although our family constantly faced major financial and medical problems, we simply did not have problems in those areas—in fact, it was just the opposite.

Within hours of my first arrival in the main Canela village, I was given a Canela name. Within a month of our family settling in the village, two families stepped up—one to adopt me as their son, and the other to adopt Jo as their daughter. We became Canelas: citizens of the village, joined with others in a complicated kinship system. I was even taken into one of the men's groups and guided through my responsibilities in the village festivals.

When it came to learning the language, it was like drinking from a fire hose. Teenagers crowded around us shouting out the Canela names for things faster than we could write them down. Once we began teaching people to read, there were so many potential students that, for the first year, we limited classes to parents of families only. Some boys who didn't make it into the reading classes stole the learn-to-read books and taught themselves. We had a profusion of translation associates. At one time we had seventeen men and women on the payroll serving as review readers, translation checkers, and typists.

As we listened to the problems enumerated by our colleagues who worked in other language groups, we realized we were very fortunate. And for years we had no idea why this was the case.

It was not until we received a letter from a Christian man in Belfast, Ireland, that we were able to account for it. The letter went something like this:

Dear Brother Jack and Sister Jo,

I just found out that you have been assigned to translate the Bible for the Canelas. I am delighted.

I once did some missionary service in Brazil. One day, as I was trekking through the jungle with some of my fellow missionaries, we stumbled upon a village we didn't know was there. It was laid out in a huge circle, with all the houses around the outside of the circle facing inward and an open plaza in the centre with paths radiating out, one to each house. From an airplane it must have looked like a gigantic wagon wheel.

The people were fierce looking. The men carried clubs and spears and none of them spoke any of the languages we knew. Frankly, we were afraid of them, and we left as quickly as we could, not daring to stay overnight in that village. Later on I found out they were called the Canela.

As the Irishman went on to tell us more about himself, we realized he had started praying for the Canela of Brazil when our parents were still teenagers! A full ten years before Jo and I were born!

He prayed faithfully for the Canela for forty years, until we finally got there—as thirty year-old linguist-translators. Then he prayed for another twenty-two years, until God's Word was translated into Canela and the Church was established. Finally, after sixty-two years of praying, the Lord took him Home, no doubt to an exceedingly great reward.

God seems to have bound Himself to act on earth mostly as His people ask Him to. He voluntarily limits Himself to work in this world mainly in response to the prayers of His children. He prepared the Canelas for our coming as an answer to that Irishman's prayers.

Jo and I spent twenty-two years of our lives talking to the Canelas about God. The Irishman from Belfast spent sixty-two years of his life talking to God about the Canelas.

Both activities were needed to give the Canelas God's Word in their language. Now God can speak to the Canelas about Himself directly from His Word.

About 2,000 language groups are still without the Word of God in the language they know best. Naturally, they are in need of well-trained, well-funded Bible translators, but prayer warriors are needed too.

And they don't even have to be Irish.

WHAT'S SO FASCINATING ABOUT BIBLE TRANSLATION?

It happened to me again the other day. A lady stopped me in church and said, "Hey, I heard your interview on the radio yesterday. You did a great job answering those questions! It was fascinating" (And she wasn't even my Mom!).

I thanked her, chatted a bit, and drove home wondering, "What is so fascinating?" I had simply answered some questions about Bible translation, linguistics, and literacy, and tossed in a few personal experience anecdotes. What's so fascinating about that?

As I thought about it, I remembered the time I was crawling on the floor of a hotel dining room, taping down the power cables for our fundraising and recruiting banquet that evening. A Rotary lunch meeting had just ended and the president of the Rotary club was chatting with our banquet tour director. The Rotarian walked over to me and asked, "I hear you learned a Brazilian indigenous language from scratch. No books, no teachers. Is that right?"

I stood up, glad for the chance to straighten my back, and said, "Yes, my wife and I worked in a translation project for twenty-two years." The president was full of questions and kept looking at me in wonder as I told him about pulling teeth and doing other medical work, learning the language and the culture, developing an alphabet, making up learn-to-read primers, training literacy teachers, translating the Bible, and training Bible teachers. He could not get enough of it.

Suddenly he glanced at his watch and said, "Look, I've got to get back to work. But, uh, um, would you mind if I shook your hand? I've never met anybody like you." I blinked in surprise, then I shook hands with him, and he walked away, looking back one more time from the doorway.

As I knelt to tape down another section of cable, I looked at my hand thinking, "The guy is right. Translators' hands really are special, but we just don't realize it. On the field, most of my friends were translators too. We got used to the extraordinary nature of our work. What was routine and common to us is exotic and fascinating to others."

In the past ten years, however, the colour of translators' hands has darkened, and I do not mean with age spots! Increasingly the fingers on the translator's keyboard are not white like mine, but black and brown—the fingers of dedicated and talented nationals, gifted and called by God to translate His Word into their own indigenous languages. They often work in committees, surrounded by Wycliffe trained facilitators—veteran translators who train them and consult with them as they work.

Peter is a native of a West African country who grew up in a village that spoke only the tribal language. His parents and the village elders noticed that he was unusually bright and quick to learn in the village school. Eventually, a government school inspector chose Peter to come with him to the city and attend a school taught in the national language. He became a Christian while studying the Bible and eventually graduated with a degree in education.

Years later, when he was a tenured teacher with a guaranteed salary, he felt God urging him to translate the Scriptures into his own tribal language. He resigned his teaching position to head up a Bible translation committee. The national translators received a modest salary through funding generated by foreign Wycliffe affiliated organizations. Eight years later, they completed the translation in their own language.

National translation committees like Peter's are working all over the world. They are great models of interdependent partnerships—translators contributing the profound knowledge of their native culture and language, with experienced Wycliffe consultants from many countries providing their expertise in linguistics, literacy, translation techniques, and in biblical culture and language. Meanwhile in North America, thousands of people are praying for these national translation committees and funding the programs through their gifts.

Out of the nearly two thousand languages that still need to have a Bible translation program started, trained and gifted bilingual nationals could probably do about sixteen hundred. They often work in cluster projects of different, but related languages, helping each other to solve translation problems common to their languages. Compared to a traditional, expatriate staffed team working under monolingual conditions, these national committees often complete a translation in half the time and at less than half the cost.

Never before in the history of the world have there been so many Bible translation project going on at the same time. The rate at which new translation projects are being started is increasing. The Holy Spirit is up to something.

God is at work. Now *that* is fascinating!

THE BIBLE TRANSLATION CONTROVERSY

While the nations gathered in Beijing to battle it out in the Olympic sports arenas, a different battle, but also with ancient traditions, raged in Jamaica. The September 2008 issue of *Christianity Today* magazine reported on the controversy.* It surrounded the ongoing translation of the Bible into Jamaican Creole, also called *patois*, which is the language spoken fluently by the vast majority of the population. While English is the official language of Jamaica, most children grow up speaking *patois/patwa* and learn English in school. Authorities do not think of it as a real language, and, therefore, the word *"patois"* is not written with a capital letter.

Letters to the newspaper editors and callers to radio phone-in programs pushed forward the usual objections to translating the Bible into *patois*—the language spoken by about two million Jamaicans: "The common language is not good enough to express the concepts of the Bible." They also urged the usual advice, "Speakers of *patois* just need to learn English better."

It seems that for centuries, whenever the Bible was translated, the new translation was criticised. Jerome translated the Bible into Latin around 400 AD. It was criticised because he had not translated it into the classical Latin used by orators and poets, but into the common, everyday Latin spoken by people on the street and at home. That is why Jerome's translation was called the Vulgate. It was vulgar, not in the sense of being indecent, but of being common.

Disapproval of new translations is routine. Even the partial Bible that my wife and I translated—with the help of gifted and trained Canela associates—was disparaged. Imagine that!

Whenever I showed the Canela Bible to Portuguese speaking Brazilian pastors, they automatically assumed that the translation in Canela was not as clear, as accurate, or as good as the Bible they used in preaching to their Portuguese speaking congregations.

I did not argue with them, but I knew from sitting in their church services that they read the archaic three-hundred-year-old Portuguese Ferreira de Almeida version, then took most of the sermon time to explain to the congregation what the passage meant before making an application. I could have told them that no one needed to explain what the Bible in Canela says—it speaks clearly right off the page.

Wherever in the world the Bible is translated into minority languages, someone will probably level criticism at it. When the Bible was translated into Plautdietsch, or Low German, the translation was criticised for not being in a language worthy to hold God's Word. People who speak fluent German do not consider Plautdietsch as a real language, just bad German. That's not true, of course. It is a perfectly legitimate language spoken by hundreds of thousands of Mennonite people as their native language.

Yet even today, church leaders in some Mennonite groups still insist on reading only the German Bible in church services, even though most of the hearers don't understand German. The rest of the service, including the preaching and praying, is in Plautdietsch.

In having their work scorned, the translators of the Bible into Jamaican *patois*, as well as the translation teams currently working in nearly two thousand other minority languages around the world, are in good company. John Wycliffe was criticised strongly for translating the Bible into English, the first major translation since Jerome's Vulgate a thousand years earlier. A contemporary historian and fellow clergyman, Henry Knighton spoke for the clergy of his day when he criticised the first translation into English under the following points:

Christ gave the Scriptures to the clergy and doctors of the Church so that they could use it to meet the needs of lay people and other weaker (uneducated) persons. John Wycliffe has now translated it into common English which has laid the Bible more open to literate laymen and women than it has formerly been to the most learned of the clergy. The jewel of the Church, hitherto the principal gift of the clergy and the divines, has now been cast abroad, and trodden under foot of swine, and is now made ever more common to laypeople.**

Henry Knighton used the wrong metaphor. The Word of God is not a jewel to be preserved in a glass case, admired, and taught by the well-educated chosen few. Jesus Himself called God's Word seed meant to be scattered generously everywhere and to sprout in prepared soil.

In the same way, the Creator made men and women in His own image, with the capacity to hear Him and communicate with Him. The Word of God can give receptive people the power to change their lives, deepen their understanding of God, and grow in love for Him.

But they must hear the Word of God first—in the language they understand best!

*Green, Jocelyn. "Translation Tiff." *Christianity Today* (September 2008): http://www.christianitytoday.com/ct/2008/september/5.15.html

**"Henry Knighton." *Encyclopedia Britannica Online* (November 14 2009): http://www.britannica.com/EBchecked/topic/320380/Henry-Knighton

SOME LITTLE KNOWN FACTS ABOUT LANGUAGES

Much criticism of Bible translation stems from a fundamental misunderstanding of the nature of language. It is not surprising that there is much confusion about languages and the need for translation. The whole issue of languages is bewildering. It is meant to be. Perplexity was the original plan. God confused the human languages at the tower of Babel. You know the story—as the babble started, the building stopped.

Here are a few surprising facts about languages to help prevent some of the criticism of Bible translation.*

Language Fact: Nearly seven thousand languages are currently spoken around the world. God loves variety. The diversity of His creation, plants, animals, and people, overwhelms us. He not only created people to develop into numerous races, but also gave us distinct personalities, making each one of us unique and different from every other human being. No wonder, then, when He created languages, He created the potential for increasing diversity.

Language Fact: The world's languages are alive and growing. Some people think a language is like a precious stone, to be kept clean and preserved unchanged. Not so. Languages, like bushes and trees, constantly change and grow. The more a language is used, the more it is likely to do so.** In the last four hundred years, the number of words in English has increased tenfold from the 60,000 words in Shakespeare's time during which the King James Authorized Version of the Bible was translated. What's more, many words have changed their meaning or become obsolete.

Language Fact: The world's languages are grouped into scores of related language families. Languages are like groves of trees, each as different from the other as poplar, palm, and pine trees. Just as each tree has a trunk, major limbs, branches, and leafy twigs, so the languages of one linguistic family are related to each other while being utterly unrelated to languages on the other trees.

Language Fact: Languages influence one another. Twigs from different trees do not change when they rub against each other, but languages do. When speakers of one language are in close contact with people speaking other languages, the languages affect each other and change even faster.

Hart Wiens is the chairman of the Wycliffe Canada board and Director of Scripture Translations for the Canadian Bible Society. He tells how the language spoken by Mennonites changed and grew, as for generations, the language was exposed to other languages.

"Russian Mennonites spoke Low Saxon, the language spoken in Holland, when they emigrated to German-speaking Prussia and later to Russia. Their language changed as it was affected by both these languages to the point where it became a distinct language, different from its ancestor language in Holland."***

Language Fact: Language is what comes out of people's mouths: inventing a way to write it down does not make it a *real* language. Scores of writing systems exist around the world, but they are not what make a language different. In Asia, for example, the Bible was translated into a language spoken by a people group that lived in four different adjacent countries. Each of these countries used a completely different writing system. At an international conference, some speakers of that language came from all four countries, looked at each other's Bibles printed in such diverse symbols, and shook their heads in confusion. Then they stood side by side and read the first Psalm aloud, each from his own Bible—in complete unison.

Language Fact: New languages are often not considered *real* languages. Just as a healthy tree drops dead leaves and sprouts new ones, so some languages become extinct while other languages develop. Many of the world's newer languages are a form of Creole, in which the new, developing language borrows words from other languages, but has its own unique grammatical system. With or without a writing system, Creoles are *real* languages.

Creole languages are often spoken in countries where a prestige language like English, French, or Spanish is the official language. Invariably, speakers of the Creole language are pressured to stop speaking that "bad English" (or French or Spanish) and speak "proper English." This is the case in Jamaica, where the official language is English and the majority language is Jamaican (*patois*).

Dr. Jo-Anne Ferreira is a lecturer in linguistics at The University of the West Indies, St. Augustine. She commented, "If Patois/Patwa is not capitalized (as for English and French), and if it is written "patois," then people will continue to ignore it as a real and proper language. The better name for the language is Jamaican, not Patois/Patwa or Jamaican Creole."

Language Fact: Every language spoken on earth today is capable of expressing the full Word of God.

*"Ethnologue: Languages of the World." SIL International. 2010.
   http://www.ethnologue.com/web.asp

**Encyclopedia Americana, Volume 10. Grolier. 1999. Quoted in the online Physics Factbook.
   http://hypertextbook.com/facts/2001/JohnnyLing.shtml

***From private correspondence with Hart Wiens

THE CASE OF THE CONSTIPATED CHURCH

Christianity is unique! It is the only major world religion that did not preserve the words of its Founder in the language in which He spoke them. Aramaic was the language commonly spoken in Palestine during Jesus life. Jesus spoke hundreds of thousands of words during His lifetime, but only a dozen words are preserved in Aramaic. Matthew, Mark, Luke, and John translated all of the Aramaic oral records of His teachings, conversations, and prayers, and translated them into Greek—a completely different language unrelated to Aramaic.

Ever since then, Christianity has depended on translation to enter thousands of cultures and languages in every nation of the world. Bible translation is, therefore, basic and foundational to the growth and health of Christianity. As a Bible translator, it disturbs me that this critical fact is not taught in Sunday schools or mentioned from the pulpit. It would stop much of the controversy about Bible translation.

No one disputes the need to translate God's Word into the *language* of the target readers and audience. The disagreement comes when godly, well-meaning people, who honour the Word of God, insist on ignoring the *culture* of the target audience.

Most of these critics do not understand what it means to translate from one culture into another culture. Metaphors, for instance, often vary widely among cultures. The translators of the 1611 King James Authorized Version, for example, tended to be quite literal, translating the metaphors common in Greek culture into English word for word, without regard to how their translation would be interpreted by people who knew only English culture.

Think of Paul's concern about the Corinthian church people being constipated. Constipated? Well, that is what it sounds like to English ears, especially today. "Ye are not straitened in us, but ye are straitened in your own bowels" (2 Cor. 6:12, KJV). Most of us know that "strait" means "constricted," and "constricted bowels" is a good description of constipation. But that is far from what Paul meant!

Greek culture considered the *bowels* to be the seat of emotion. English culture, on the other hand, thinks of the *heart* as the place of feelings and affections. The Canelas talk of the *ear*, other cultures of the *liver* or the *throat*, etc. Weymouth's version goes half way when he translates, "There is no narrowness in our love to you, the narrowness is in your own feelings" (WNT). "Narrowness" still sounds unnatural to us, but at least he abandoned the "bowels" and uses "love" and "feelings." Using our English culture's metaphor, we could translate it, "Our hearts are open to you, but yours are closed to us." Without the metaphor, it is simply, "We love you, but you don't love us."

When Jo and I translated Matthew 24:41 into Canela, we had a similar problem. Jesus foretells the end times, "Two women shall be grinding at the mill; the one shall be taken, and the other left." The mill used at that time was made of two flat stones.

Our problem was that the Canelas do not grind grain, and the local stones are chunks of lava rock—useless for grinding. We had to discard the "grinding" metaphor. Wanting a clear, dynamic translation, we asked ourselves, "What is there in the Canela culture that would give a similar picture, and that would carry the same meaning as the original?"

Every morning during rice harvest, pairs of women pound rice to separate the kernels from the hulls. The rice is in a large mortar—a hollowed hardwood log standing on end. The pestles are metre-long clubs. We used to wake up every morning to their rhythmic THUNK—thonk, THUNK—thonk. If one woman disappeared, no one would even need to look since the single THUNK—...., THUNK—.... sound alone would carry the message.

"But you are changing the Word of God!" some folk have told me. Yes, in a way I am. But I am in good company. The first translators, Matthew, Mark, Luke, and John, also chose different words as they focused not only on the language but also on the way of life of their readers. Matthew wrote his Gospel keeping Jewish culture in mind, while Luke and Mark wrote for people in the Greco-Roman culture.

Dr. Wayne Dye is an International Consultant for Scripture Use in SIL—Wycliffe's field partner. He points out the startling differences.* In two parallel passages describing the same scene—Matthew 16:13 and Mark 8:27—Matthew translates Jesus as saying, "Whom do men say that I the *Son of Man* am?" while Mark simply translates, "Whom do men say that I am?" (KJV).

Did Mark leave out something that Jesus said? Yes, he did! He left out an obscure third person term that Matthew's Jewish readers would know referred to the Messiah. But Mark was willing, under the guidance of God's Holy Spirit, to leave out that ambiguous meaning to make sure he did not confuse his non-Jewish readers.

Even more startling is how Matthew, Mark, and Luke each changed what Jesus actually said in Aramaic to fit the cultural understanding of their audiences. Dr. Dye writes, "In many passages, Matthew reported Jesus as talking about the *Kingdom of Heaven*. In every parallel passage, Mark and Luke translated this as *Kingdom of God*. Mark and Luke never use the phrase *Kingdom of Heaven*. The cultural difference explains it. Matthew's Jewish readers would understand *Heaven* to mean the place where God reigns. Mark and Luke's Greek readers would have thought of the *Kingdom of Heaven* as the home of their Greek pantheon, a rather tacky group of gods and goddesses—a concept totally different from Jesus' original meaning."

Matthew, Mark, and Luke chose terms to fit not only the *language* spoken by their readers, but also the *culture* of their respective audiences to produce a dynamic, culture sensitive, meaning-based translation.

Bible translators for all the world's nearly seven thousand languages and cultures today need to follow the biblical examples set by these first translators. To translate into the readers' *language* but ignore their *culture* spreads needless confusion and misunderstanding.

*Private correspondence in 2007 with Dr. T. Wayne Dye about his book, *The Bible Translation Strategy* (Dallas: Wycliffe Bible Translators, 1980)

WHEN IS ENOUGH?

"Grandpa, that was just a short one," my triplet granddaughters tend to complain, "Tell us another story." I have been telling or reading bedtime stories to our grandchildren for nearly twenty years and no matter how long the story is, or how many I tell, they always want another one—and not just because they want to put off going to sleep! It's human to want more of something good. But when is enough?

In the summer of 2009, for instance, our whole family traveled through Brazil and, after spending a few days in the Canela village, Jo cried when we had to leave. That was understandable: she wanted more time with them. But she also cried the day we left the village after living with them periodically for twenty-two years. When is enough?

After spending nearly six weeks with his California cousins, our nine-year old grandson, Aidan, said a tearful goodbye and exclaimed, "It's not fair. How come God gives you something really good, and then, just when you really like it, He yanks it away?"

Good question, Aidan. Whether it is a bedtime story or a great friendship, a weeklong honeymoon or a fifty-year marriage, it is never enough. We always want more. C. S. Lewis, Christian writer and apologist, recognized this when he wrote, "If I find in myself a desire which no experience in this world can satisfy, the most probable explanation is that I was made for another world."*

That's just it. We *are* made for another world. Pierre Teilhard, a wise philosopher-priest, explained it like this, "We are not human beings having a spiritual experience: but spiritual beings having a human experience."**

Exactly! Just as a tourist enjoys visiting the ruins of ancient cities and says, "I love visiting, but I wouldn't want to live here," so we are tourists on planet earth, enjoying the visit, but knowing that we would never want to live here forever.

When our Brazilian friends invite us to dinner, they offer us appetizers, a variety of delicious little savouries called *salgadinhas*. Although it is hard not to fill up on the tiny pies, the little fish balls, and small bits of meat wrapped in savoury dough, their only purpose is to *abrir o apetite*, literally to "open the appetite." So it is with all the good things God gives us here on earth. They are just to stimulate our appetite, not to satisfy us. They merely prepare us to enjoy the real meal.

Right now we love and enjoy many things—friendship, marriage, family, good food, the wonders of nature, the joy of accomplishing great work, good stories, music, praising God, and researching and studying to satisfy our curiosity. But these hundreds of things that bring us pleasure during this life are merely appetizers, not the real meal. For that completely satisfying heavenly banquet, we will need to wait—with great expectation.

In our current affluence, it is easy to enjoy many kinds of good things. Some retired Christian men and women in good health go from one enjoyable leisure activity to another. For some it is golf, others like fishing, and others become absorbed in sports or hobbies. These activities are good clean fun—great appetizers.

But I wonder what would happen if we upgraded these retirement and vacation activities from being merely good clean fun, to being enjoyable things that also build God's Kingdom?

I often challenge my friends (and myself!) to do this upgrade by quoting the words of Jesus, "Seek first his (God's) Kingdom and his righteousness, and all these things will be given to you as well" (Matt. 6:33, NIV).

Most of us enjoy our health, our affluence, and our freedom to travel, and we thank God for them. But we could leverage these gifts into meeting desperate needs in this world. I know of some families who use the money and time they budget for vacation to take short work trips to the mission field. Some retired folk, instead of going on another cruise, spend extended time overseas to help mission projects in any way they can. Others visit a missionary they pray for and support. Some stay in their home country and donate their skills and expertise to work as volunteers in organizations set up to meet the needs of the poor, the sick, the elderly, the lonely, and the disadvantaged.

These are more than just more interesting and enjoyable experiences. They extend God's Kingdom; they are personal eye-openers and sometimes even life-changers. Those who get personally involved tell how good it feels to know God used them to meet deep needs. They tell of the difficulties they overcame and the unique experiences they enjoyed—enjoyments that are on a whole different level than an appetizer.

But, sadly, for every person that does get personally involved, there are a dozen who have never tried it.

My advice? "Try it, you'll like it."

You may enjoy it. But it will still be just an appetizer for the Great Banquet where we will finally be fully satisfied. Finally no more saying goodbye. Finally no more stories that are too short.

Finally, it will be enough.

*Lewis, C.S. *Mere Christianity*. Harper Collings Publishers, 2001.

**"Inspirational Quotes: Words of Wisdom." Reiki Healing Power. http://www. reikihealingpower.com/quotes.htm

THE TEACHER WHO MADE A U-TURN

"I can't believe my eyes! I can't believe my ears!" the Brazilian teacher exclaimed to me. It was her first visit to the Canela village, and it was neither the sight of bare-chested men relay-racing with a heavy log, nor the sound of the bare-breasted women singing in a dancing line on the plaza that overwhelmed her. She was struck by something far more important.

She had occasionally tried to teach a few Canela young people to read in Portuguese when they made an extended visit to a nearby Brazilian town. She found their progress extremely slow and began to think that all Canelas were mentally handicapped. Many of the townspeople shared the same opinion. Just like the Canela adults she sometimes saw in the streets, her students spoke Portuguese reluctantly, making many errors, and had obvious trouble understanding everything Portuguese-speaking Brazilians were saying.

"Today in this village," she told me, "I got a totally different picture. All morning I was amazed by the Canela adults, teens, and children! They were chattering away animatedly, not at all like the silent, mumbling, and confused-looking people they are in town."

"Would you like to hear some of the Canelas read?" I asked. She had endured listening to Canela students and their attempts to read before, but when she heard children, teens, and adults reading Canela fluently, with expression and obvious delight, she said, "I can't believe it! My opinion has taken a U-turn today! I can hardly wait to tell my friends and colleagues in town." Then she whispered to me, "No sign of anyone having mental disabilities."

But she was due for another shock. I picked up a novel in Portuguese and handed it to one of the teenage boys who was standing around and asked him to read it. He opened the book randomly and started reading—reading Portuguese, and reading fluently.

The teacher was astounded! "Where did he learn to read Portuguese that well?" she asked, knowing he had never been in *her* class. "He's never been to school in town," I replied. "He taught himself to read Portuguese after he learned to read Canela. He may not understand all the words he is reading since he doesn't speak much Portuguese yet, but the words he is familiar with come out fluently."

The teacher learned several things that day: 1) The mother language is the natural context in which to learn to read. 2) After learning to read in the mother language, it is much easier for the student to learn to read in a language with which he is less familiar. 3) Judging people's identities and mental abilities accurately can best be done within the context of their own culture and language.

Mr. Koichiro Matsuura, Director-General of UNESCO said something similar in his 2009 message for *International Mother Language Day*, recognized on February 21.*

"Languages," he said, "form part of the identity of individuals and peoples." He then focused on the importance of the mother language in education.

"Links between multilingual education (involving the mother-tongue, national languages, and international languages), *Education for All*, and the *Millennium Development Goals* constitute the pillars of any sustainable-development strategy."

He also emphasized that during the last ten years, since the establishment of International Mother *Language Day*, people are finally beginning to realize the importance of mother tongue languages. "A growing number of increasingly diverse stakeholders in governmental organizations and civil society acknowledge that languages are central to all forms of social, economic, and cultural life." And *to spiritual life* I would add.

For centuries Christians have been translating God's Word into other languages. The importance of the mother language in cross-cultural missions and evangelism was emphatically and clearly restated in *The Amsterdam 2000 Declaration: A Charter for Evangelism in the 21st*

Century, recognized and approved by twelve thousand evangelists and leaders from around the world:

"The Bible is indispensable. . . . Thus we must proclaim and disseminate the Holy Scriptures in the heart language (mother language) of all those whom we are called to evangelize and disciple. . . ."

One day at an international conference, some of us translators were swapping stories. One translator told this story:

"We had been assigned to translate the Bible for a conservative indigenous people group that had been Christianized in Spanish fifty years earlier. Sunday church services were conducted in Spanish with the men sitting on one side, and women sitting on the other, as was their custom. The women's side was awash in colour, while the men's side was marked by their traditional white cowboy hats. They never took these white hats off, even in church, except when the pastor said, 'Let us pray.'

"One day I presented the indigenous pastor with the first passage from the Bible ever translated into his language. The next Sunday, the congregation stood, as usual, for the reading of the Bible. The pastor began to read the passage, not in Spanish, but in their own mother language. He had read only a few verses when, like a great white wave, every man took off his sombrero."

No wonder. For the first time in their lives they heard God speak directly to their hearts!

*Koichiro Matsuura. "Message for International Mother Language Day." United Nations Educational, Scientific and Cultural Organization. 21 Feb. 2009.

http://unesdoc.unesco.org/images/0017/001799/179967e.pdf

THE CASE FOR MOTHER-TONGUE TRANSLATORS

My wife and I traveled to Brazil over forty years ago to begin our Bible translation ministry among the Canela people. We learned the language and the culture, developed an alphabet, and taught the Canelas to read, write, and do arithmetic. Then, with their help, we translated a large part of the Bible. Nearly twenty-five years after our arrival, we completed the project, and left behind the newly published Scriptures and a young Church. Yes, it took a very long time!

How things have changed since then! The massive improvements in the world of Bible translation have been exciting, positive, and incredibly encouraging. Praise God!

Today, for example, Bible translators are completing translation projects in indigenous languages in a much shorter time and at a smaller cost. What's more, the quality of the translation is better than ever!

What factors are responsible for this marvellous change?

Obviously, computers play a big part. Dictionary-making programs have revolutionized this time consuming task. Translated material does not need to be typed, proofed, and retyped, saving time and improving quality.

Also, in the last seventy years, Wycliffe and its field partner organizations have accumulated a wealth of first-hand knowledge about linguistics and Bible translation. The current generation of Bible translators benefit immensely from this knowledge through excellent training and experienced at-their-elbow consultants.

The greatest reason, however, for the exciting improvement in worldwide Bible translation is neither better computers nor greater knowledge, but the translators themselves. In the past, foreigners, like my wife and I, did almost all the translations. We worked with uneducated people groups that were fluent only in their own language.

Today, however, linguistic surveyors estimate that of the people groups that still need the Bible translated into their language, 80 percent have at least some well-educated people in their populations—people who are fluent in other languages beside their own mother tongue. What's more, often these educated, multilingual people are Christians whom God is calling to translate His Word into their own mother tongue. Once they are trained in Bible translation principles and techniques, funded by sponsors, and surrounded by experienced consultants, they are on the fast track to producing high quality Bible translations.

Think of the advantages these mother-tongue translators have:

> They already know and understand both the language and the culture. It is far easier and much faster to translate accurately into your own language than into a foreign language you have learned.

> They already live in the country and among the people—a vital advantage in those nations where access by foreigners is extremely difficult. (Expatriates spend huge amounts of time and money in travel, passports, visas, inoculations, and to provide special schooling for their children on the field.)

> Once the translation project is completed by mother-tongue translators, it is seen by the people group as something that belongs to them, not something foreign introduced from outside.

So how successful are these projects staffed by nationals?

Three projects in Africa and four in South Asia took an average of twelve years to complete—about half the time it took my wife and me to finish a traditional project.* The average cost per project was about one-third of the cost of our traditional project. In just one twelve month period starting in mid-2008, 4,300,000 people, from thirty different language groups received the Scriptures in their languages for the first time. Trained, well-funded mother-tongue translators, assisted by experienced Wycliffe advisors and consultants, were responsible for most of these projects.

What does it take, besides consistent prayer, for a mother-tongue Bible translation project to succeed?

Mother-tongue translators need to be gifted, prepared, and called to work together as a translation committee. This is God's job.

The translators need to be fully trained and provided with experienced consultants to help them solve translation and administrative problems, and to assure the final translation is of high quality. This is Wycliffe's job.

Financial supporters and sponsors need to fund the translation project. This is the Church's job.

In round numbers, nearly twenty-five hundred languages still need their own translations of the Bible. Of these, about five hundred languages are spoken by people groups that are still relatively uneducated and monolingual. Translation projects under these conditions need to be staffed by well-trained outsiders. They will use computers and train the indigenous speakers to produce an accurate and smooth flowing translation.

The other nearly two thousand languages of the world, however, are spoken by people groups with at least some educated people among the population—presenting a good possibility of developing some mother-tongue translators. God has gifted and called nationals to be trained to do this work, and Wycliffe is ready to train and prepare them. But in many cases, the Church has delayed the start of the work because she has not yet provided the essential funding.

National believers obviously want the Word of God in their own language! They often help build translation centres and provide some of the food needed by the translation committees and their families. But the cost of computers, equipment, travel, training, and living expenses is so high, it simply cannot be provided locally. This funding must come from individuals and churches in North America and elsewhere.

Before my wife and I left for Brazil, and during each furlough, we raised all the funds we needed to live and work. We shared the vision with our friends, relatives, and churches in North America and invited them to join our support team. National translators living in relative poverty cannot do that. They depend on others to raise the funding they need.

Wycliffe's home organizations and their partner organizations now work harder than ever to alert God's people to the teamwork needed.

The Church at home has the ability, the responsibility, and privilege to help fund the national translators. For their part, the nationals are best qualified to do the translation.

And as a writer and speaker, I am happy to do my part.

*"Global PartnerLink 2008 Annual Report." Global PartnerLink. http://www.globalpartnerlink. ca/fCMSBackend/imgRoot//homepageImages/Annual_report_2008_new.pdf

A TICKLISH SUBJECT

My wife has learned not to use a certain four-letter word with me. Instead of asking me to *wait* until she is ready, she says *read* or *walk* or *play* or *work*—all acceptable four-letter words. Just don't tell me to *wait*.

Most action-oriented people like me hate having to wait. Yet making His people wait is one of the things God does most consistently. We pray. We wait. We receive. What is it with the time lag that is so important to God?

We can find a clue to the answer on the bottoms of our feet—the spots where most of us are ticklish. We can rub or lightly scratch the bottoms of our own feet with little or no reaction. But if someone else does this, the reaction is instantaneous and explosive. I learned to nap with my shoes on when there were small grandkids in the house.

Author J. Ingram described a study of this tickle phenomenon in his book, *The Theatre of the Mind.** The tickle effect is provoked only where the action is not under the control of the one being tickled. The researcher built a simple device on which a subject would place her naked foot. She would then jiggle a handle which activated a thin rod that lightly scraped the bottom of her feet. This provoked little or no reaction. When someone else jiggled the handle, however, the reaction was immediate.

The researcher then activated a time delay. The subject would jiggle the handle, but instead of the tickle rod immediately touching her foot, there was a delay of one to five seconds. When the tickle rod moved there was an immediate tickle reaction.

The researcher concluded that some doubt was essential before a tickle effect could be produced. The tickle effect can only come about when the initiating action is not fully under the control of the one being tickled. Even when there was no other person involved, a time delay of unknown length between action and result would set off the tickle effect. What's more, the longer the delay, the stronger the effect. No doubt: no tickle. More doubt: more tickle.

We have all asked God to do something for us we could not do for ourselves. We have often received positive answers to these prayers. But we have even more often experienced delays between our prayer and God's answer or provision. Some of us are in the waiting stage right now.

The eternal God appears to use earthly time to produce a stronger faith effect in us.

On the afternoon of His resurrection day, for example, Jesus appeared to His disciples and breathed on them, saying, "Receive the Holy Spirit."

Instantly there was the sound of a rushing mighty wind, the room was shaken, and flames of fire appeared above the heads of the disciples and they were filled with the Holy Spirit.

No, that is not what happened.

Nothing happened at all. Jesus disappeared and the disciples remained without the Holy Spirit for nearly six weeks. Uncertainties crept in. Peter and some others returned to fishing. Even after Jesus appeared to them again and ascended to heaven right before their eyes, they had to wait for another ten days. They came together to encourage each other to wait and pray expectantly. Finally, a full fifty days after Jesus' statement, they finally received the Holy Spirit.

Why all the waiting and struggling against uncertainty and doubt? The long wait was needed in order to produce an enormous faith effect. In the end, their faith was so strong it could not be shaken.

Jo and I once prayed and waited for five years for God to reopen the door for us to return to the Canela village to complete the translation project. They were the worst years of our lives. Like Thomas, I doubted—a lot!

But after God took us through that waiting period, our faith was much stronger. We completed the project in seven, intensive, highly focused years. No regular furlough, just work sessions, still meeting opposition, but overcoming the problems with a growing faith in a strong God.

I still do not like waiting—not even at a traffic light. When going to appointments, I make sure I carry a book with me so I can at least read in the waiting room.

Some things, like growing a baby in the womb or growing our faith, simply take time. The apostle Paul writes about this pregnancy of faith in Romans 8:24-25: "Waiting does not diminish us; any more than waiting diminishes a pregnant mother. We are enlarged in the waiting. . . . The longer we wait, the larger we become, and the more joyful our expectancy" (*The Message*).

The less control and the longer the wait, the greater will be the result, whether in a tickle giggle, or in God faith.

*J. Ingram. *The Theatre of the Mind: Raising the Curtain of Consciousness*. 1st edition, 2005. Canada: Harper Collins. http://www.harpercollins.ca/book/index.aspx?isbn=9780002006699

A HORROR PREVENTED

My wife and I were shocked and aghast to hear the horror story during our initial training forty-five years ago.

After sacrificing three decades of their lives to learn an unwritten language and translate a part of the Bible into it, the translation team discovered the indigenous group was not interested in reading the Book. In fact, few wanted to learn to read. Ten years later, those Scripture books were still stored in a warehouse. The team made some of those passages available as audio recordings, but most of the visible results of years of sacrificial work and great financial cost stayed sealed in boxes on the shelf. What's more, we were assured, theirs was not an isolated case.

Jo and I determined to do everything we could to avoid such a horror. We prayed a lot and asked for advice from fellow translators and a knowledgeable anthropologist. Right from the start, we introduced the Canelas to the concept of the printed word and the delight of reading. With little privacy in our home, Canelas sat and listened to me reading to my family in the evenings. Although they did not understand a word of our English, they noticed our daughters' and Jo's obvious enjoyment. When the girls learned to read, Canelas would often see all five of us reading our own books, chuckling to ourselves, or sharing stories or passages with each other.

We brought in stacks of National Geographic magazines and made them available for Canela visitors to look at on the porch. It took weeks before they began to understand that those flat two-dimensional, page-sized splashes of colour represented full size, three-dimensional people and animals. Growing up in a literate society, we had seen pictures since we were babies and interpreted pictures before we could talk, but the Canelas had to start learning this as adults.

One day, I heard an excited voice from the porch, "Look at this black panther!" I looked up just in time to see an old man ripping a page out of the magazine and handing it to his friend, sharing it with him the way he would share a tobacco leaf from his bundle. Time to teach about the permanence of books; the leaves need to stay in the bundle.

Long before we started translating the Bible, we developed learn-to-read booklets and taught some Canelas to read and to be literacy teachers. We also published a series of small reading booklets transcribed from tape recorded traditional stories and legends. The newly literate Canelas loved them.

The Canelas love music and drama, so we capitalized on those cultural values. With the help of an expert ethno-musicologist we set Scripture verses to Canela music. They were singing parts of the Canela Bible years before the Scriptures were published.

After the evening classes, we frequently checked the accuracy of the translated Bible stories by having the students act them out. You can imagine the enactment of Jesus' story of the sower and the soils (Matt. 13:3-23). A big, strong Canela is the sower. He picks up some little kids and "sows" them here and there. They fall to the ground, lie there for a while like a seed on the ground, and then slowly get up, simulating growth. Soon they begin to suffer the consequences of rocky soil, or weeds, or other young men carrying them off, cawing loudly. Hilarious! We heard that they even performed on the central plaza in front of hundreds of other Canelas. This was a great stimulus to people to read the Bible to find more stories.

We decided to translate not just a New Testament, but a more understandable partial Bible. When it was published, the Canelas started reading Genesis on page one and read through the abbreviated chronological Old Testament. When they were a quarter of the way through the Book, they finally got to read about Jesus and were prepared to see Him as the culmination of the whole story.

We also pushed Bible memory, first of all, in order to help the Canelas get to know the basic themes of the Bible. Beyond that, we also wanted to give them an opportunity to earn a copy of the new Bible by memorizing large parts of it. When we left the Canela village to return to Canada, every home had at least one fluent reader and a Canela Bible.

A year and a half later, we returned for a visit and took photos of the four hundred Canelas who happened to be in the village at that time. We printed those photos, added the names, and gave them out one by one to Christian friends all over North America who solemnly promised to pray for "their" Canela every day. Even now, seventeen years later, I still get notes from some of those prayer partners telling me they are still praying in spite of the fact that the child whose picture they have is now probably a mother with many children.

According to our anthropologist friend, the Canelas' current motivating drive is for education. Teachers are still using the original Canela primer booklets to get children started in reading, and then they gradually switch over to lessons in Portuguese. Trained bilingual Canela teachers staff the village school. Some young people now ride trucks into the nearest town to get further education, returning to the village for weekends. One young Canela woman, who was just a baby when we left, is completing high school and plans to go to university to become a doctor.

Most of the chiefs who were appointed to lead the village in the past twenty years are Bible readers. Some of them worked with us as translation helpers, others were graduates of the evening Bible classes. We heard numerous stories of people reading the Canela Bible aloud in their homes or in semi-public locations. During our visit this past summer, we repeated the "Earn a Bible through memorization" offer and were mobbed by the current leadership eager to get a memory booklet.

God led us to do all those creative things to promote reading in the Canela village. They turned out to be the right things to do, in our particular situation, at that time.

Thank God, the Canela story is not a horror story.

OIL ON TROUBLED WATERS

My first published article ended in a near personal disaster.

The editor of a small denominational magazine asked me, a young pastor of a small church, to write an article. It concerned a doctrinal position that set the denomination apart from mainstream evangelicals. I accepted the invitation. In the article, I asked some provocative questions, proposed a biblical alternative to the traditional doctrinal position, and presented what I thought were excellent arguments and proofs.

Unfortunately as a rookie writer, I didn't know about word limits and overshot the maximum. The editor cut my article down to size by simply printing my provocative questions and opinions, but cutting out all my reasons and evidence!

The ensuing uproar was inevitable. The editor received a record number of letters, and phones rang off the hook at the denomination's head office. The leadership called me on the carpet to present my case, threatening to defrock me if my explanation was not satisfactory. Defrock—ecclesiastical language for revoking my ordination as a minister. No more *Reverend* Popjes. I escaped this fate by a hair and learned a vital lesson—know the word limit and stick to it.

Forty-five years later, I am still writing, publishing, and causing occasional uproars. One such was started by the column *A Horror Prevented* which was a testimonial of what Jo and I had done to promote literacy among the Canela. I received a greater than usual number of reader responses. Most of the responses from the general readership joined me in thanking God for an obviously successful literacy program; however, many of my fellow-Bible translators responded by waving red caution flags and shouting, "Yes, but . . . !"

What troubled my Bible translating colleagues was this implication. If only all two thousand current translation programs, and the twenty-three hundred programs yet to start, would implement the *Popjes Sure-Fire Formula for Literacy Success* as outlined in that column, all would be well. Twenty years later, thousands of missionary newsletters would praise God for illiterate indigenous societies totally transformed into educated, Bible reading communities.

In hindsight, I saw that readers could pick up that implication. It is not what I intended. Bringing change to a society is far more complicated and unpredictable than what my column led some people to believe. Here are some reasons: God made every one of us unique. This means every translation team differs from every other translation team. In the same way, each language group has its own distinctive cultural, social, and linguistic situation. What's more, these situations change over time, even within the same group. God loves variety, which is why every snowflake is unique. So is every translation and literacy program. There simply is no *one-size-fits-all* literacy solution.

Another aspect to consider is the fact that God is sovereign. He gives us the privilege to work with Him to accomplish His work on earth, but He is still in charge of the timing and the results. What's more, He has given every individual a free will. People in indigenous societies can choose to become educated or not. God has given them that ability and that right. We can only work, pray, and hope they will choose the path that will be the best for them in the end.

Although there is no *one-size-fits-all* format, there are some basic universals to being an agent of change. One is the need to show up. If you want to see an indigenous society change, you need to be there and live in that culture, love the people around you, and model the behaviour over an extended time. It is what Jesus did when He came to earth. He modeled a sinless life, revealed God to people, and showed mankind what love really looked like.

In hindsight, we now know our program was not as good as it could have been. We were under-supported financially in our first term of service in Brazil, and we often felt restricted in our ministry. But God, being in charge, used even this problem to bring about some good results. Since we could not afford to travel back and forth to the missions centre every three or four months as our colleagues did, we had six to seven month-long sessions. We had little contact with consultants, and we often spun our wheels academically, but we did learn to speak the language quickly and fluently. We also built very strong relationships with the Canelas. We were there, we showed up, and God blessed us, and consequently, our ministry.

Which clarifies the most important basic universal fact—God blesses people, not programs.

IT'S A NEW ONE!

Scene 1: 1981, in North America

In churches, prayer meetings, Sunday schools and homes, tens of thousands of people pray for the thirty-three hundred people groups around the world that still do not have even one passage of Scripture translated into their own language:

"Send out Bible translators. Raise up financial supporters. Open doors to these people groups. Speak to hearts through Your Word as it is translated. Bring these people groups into your Kingdom."

Scene 2: 1981, a translation centre in Belem, Brazil

Twenty Bible translators pray earnestly for a dozen people groups in their area:

"Please open the way for us to return to the villages. It's been three years since we have had any contact with them. Oh, God, we miss them so! Change the government policy that forbids us to visit these villages. In the meantime, prepare the hearts of the Apalai, the Apinaje, the Canela, and the other people groups to obey the small portions of Your Word that have been translated."

Scene 3: 1981, a Canela village in Brazil

Jaco, a young man, swings in his hammock in a palm thatch house. He is reading a pack of stapled together pages, a carbon copy of the first draft of the book of Luke. After a while he puts the papers down and begins to talk to himself.

"I've been reading these pages every day for many months. Three years ago, I helped to translate them. When am I going to stop just reading them? When will I believe them and obey them?"

He climbs out of the hammock, walks out to the backyard, and looks up into the clear blue sky and says,

"*Cojkwa kam Inxu cati*—Great Father in the sky—This is me, my name is Jaco. You don't know me, but I've been reading Your papers and according to them I am bad, very bad. I am sorry. Please don't remember my badness. Please help me to live right from now on."

Scene 4: 1981, Heaven

The usual multitude of angels is singing and praising God around His throne. A large number of angels lean over the parapets of heaven to observe the people on earth. Suddenly one of the angelic watchers holds up both hands and shouts, "Stop! Listen!"

Heaven falls silent as the angels listen intently. They hear a voice from earth, "*Cojkwa kam Inxu cati . . .*"

The angels look at each other astonished. "We've never heard that language here before. This is not just a repentant sinner. It's a new one—the first one in his people group!"

Instantly a swelling cheer of joy resounds throughout heaven! Thousands more angels, whole choirs of them, come flying from every part of heaven carrying their instruments with them. A musical extravaganza of overwhelming joy begins.

In the scribe room, the recording angel checks his list, makes a mark alongside "Canela" and says, "Three-thousand, two-hundred and ninety-nine to go."

During the past thirty years, the angelic choirs heard words of repentance in a thousand languages never before heard in heaven, for the first time. They are celebrating with joyful musical extravaganzas more often than ever before in the history of the world.

The recording angel checks off names at an accelerating pace. On his seven-thousand-name list of nations, ethnic groups and languages, about two-thousand remain.

May God's people on earth keep praying fervently, keep giving generously, and keep volunteering their lives to translate the Good News into every single language in the world.

SEE DICK AND JANE RUN— TO MISSIONS

World-renowned palaeontologist Dr. Phil Currie was the dinosaur curator of the Royal Tyrrell Museum whose research helped Alberta's Dinosaur Provincial Park achieve UNESCO world heritage status. He is a university professor and a world expert on theropods who even has a dinosaur named after him.*

So when did he decide his life's work? When, as a six-year-old, he found a plastic dinosaur in a cereal box.

I am not surprised. Anecdotes abound of young children being impacted in ways that set the course of their careers and their lives. My ninety-five-year-old mother's memory is sharp and clear, especially about things in the distant past. As she reminisced with me about things that happened when I was a child in the Netherlands, she mentioned that, at age seven, I told her I might become a missionary.

Although I do not remember that incident, I know I was thinking about missions while reading a series of storybooks about the work of Dutch missionaries in Indonesia, a former Dutch colony.

I remember reading of a young Indonesian orphan boy about my own age who was taken home by a sadistic uncle who treated him as a slave and beat him viciously for almost any reason. I knew what a well-deserved spanking with the *matteklopper*, "wicker carpet beater" felt like. The illustration of the native boy writhing naked on the ground while the brutal uncle flogged him mercilessly with a bamboo stick sent shivers down my seven-year-old spine.

I realized even then, that to bring a change to that poor boy, to his heartless uncle, and the rest of the people in that village, they needed to learn about a God of love. I was happy to read that a missionary came to tell them.

I became a Christian as a young teenager in Canada. The pastor once asked us at a youth meeting, "Have any of you ever considered becoming a pastor or missionary?" I was amazed that no one said a word. Being shy (at that time) I did not say anything either, but I mentally answered, "Yes, of course! Since Jesus gave His life for me, shouldn't I give my life for him?"

The Bible comes on strong about teaching God's principles to our children. "Impress them on your children. Talk about them when you sit at home and when you walk along the road, when you lie down and when you get up" (Deut. 6:7, NIV).

How well do today's Christian families live up to that standard? Most of us teach our children to love God and to be honest, hardworking, and helpful to others. But many consider Christ's final command to evangelize the world and disciple the nations a low priority and never talk about it.

Urbana conference speaker Dr. Tony Campolo was delighted to see hundreds of young people stand up and give their lives to missions after his challenging speech. A few weeks later, his delight turned to despair as he received scores of letters from these young people telling him their parents did not want them to become missionaries.**

In contrast, when my wife, Jo, was born, her mother privately dedicated her to God and quietly prayed for decades that she would become a missionary. Her mom did not tell her until Jo had completed Bible school and was ready to leave Biola University to take a missionary medicine course.

We Christian parents need to put a high priority on missions and pray that God will use our children in worldwide missions. We need to expose them to missions through books, stories, videos, hospitality to "real live" missionaries, and, when possible, through short term mission trips.

We also need to remember that when a child becomes a Christian, the Holy Spirit moves into his or her body to live out the life of Christ. There is no *Lite* version of the Holy Spirit, He is there in full strength and is as ready to work in our children's lives as He is in the life of the most mature pastor.

Parents need to be willing to send their children, and their grandchildren, to the far corners of the earth for years at a time. I thank God that my parents and Jo's mom had that attitude. At the celebration in the village when we distributed the Canela partial Bible, our parents said,

"It was hard to see them go. We hurt for them in all their troubles and stresses. We missed them terribly all those years. But now, when we see the Canelas hugging the Bible our kids translated, it was worth it. Oh yes, it was worth it!"

Churches and mission agencies need to work together creatively to bring the vision of cross-cultural foreign missions to children. Kids need gripping stories, live missionaries, and missions lessons in Children's Church.

Hmm, and how about plastic figurines in cereal boxes?

*"Royal Tyrell Museum." Tyrell Museum. 2010: http://www.tyrrellmuseum.com
**This story is the basis of the twenty-two minute Wycliffe video "The Canela Investment"

✦ COLUMN 15 ✦
TRADITIONS TO BE CHANGED

As the crowd waved palm branches and shouted praises, Jesus rode a donkey into Jerusalem a few days before his arrest and execution. We celebrate this event as Palm Sunday. The apostles, however, seemed to have had better things to do during subsequent decades than commemorate this event.

There is no evidence that, for the first three hundred years of Christianity, any church, anywhere in the world, ever held a Palm Sunday celebration.* Eventually, churches began to commemorate the event as the start of Holy Week, and for seventeen centuries, the tradition spread and established itself in churches all over the world.

Traditions are to a group what habits are to an individual. We all know how easy it is to start a habit: just do something repeatedly and regularly, and soon it becomes a habit. Organizations and families can start a tradition in the same way.

Habits and traditions can be useful. We cannot drive a car, perform heart surgery, or get to the next level in a video game without practicing certain actions repeatedly until they become habits. Similarly, organizations cannot run effectively unless they establish a good set of actions which the staff practices regularly until they become an organizational tradition.

Habits can be as healthy as a brisk early morning walk, or as destructive as a drug addiction. A collection of actions becomes a habit; a collection of habits becomes a character. Clearly, we need to be careful about the habits we acquire. Bad ones are hard to break. Just ask the hunt-and-peck keyboardist who is trying to break the old bad habit of looking down at her keyboard before she can develop the new and better habit of touch-typing.

Personal habits are not sacred. Nor are group traditions—not even long-standing church traditions. A keyboardist may have hunted and pecked on a keyboard for years, but that is no reason for her to continue this habit. The same principle applies to the traditions of our North American evangelical churches.

Although most evangelical churches are not based as heavily on liturgy and centuries-old traditions as other denominations, we evangelicals still need to audit our old traditions and consider building some new ones. Here are four somewhat related traditions that could stand some change:

1. Traditionally, we have a lot of *preaching about* God's Word, but little public *reading of* God's Word. A recent church service I attended featured thirty-eight minutes of preaching about a number of biblical texts, but only thirty-eight seconds of straight, unadorned Bible reading. Yes, I checked it on my watch.

I recently read the book of Job in *The Message* version aloud to my wife during our regular morning devotional time. Although I had read Job dozens of times, reading it aloud impressed both of us with the whole drama of that story. Reading the Bible translated into ordinary language has a power all its own. The apostle Paul commanded his disciple Timothy to read the Bible aloud in public, along with preaching and teaching (1 Tim. 4:13). Hmm, reading, preaching, teaching. How about dividing these activities into three equal time slots? Sounds like a good tradition to me!

2. Traditionally, we put a lot of emphasis on *talking to people about God* and little emphasis on *talking to God about people*. Our tradition is to be a preacher instead of a priest, whose role is to pray for people. Pastors preach to congregations. Congregations talk with their neighbours, friends, and co-workers about Christ. But what about prayer? Is prayer an agenda item for every meeting? Is prayer taught, promoted, and practiced in every program and department of the church? Is there a pastor of prayer on staff?

A widow we know is unique. She spreads hundreds of photos of family, friends and missionaries on her bed every morning. She goes into her bedroom many times throughout the day, kneels down, and prays for some of them. She does not go to sleep at night until she has prayed for them all, and the photos are back in the box. What a habit! But in a church that has a true prayer tradition, she would not be unique, just one of many.

3. And speaking of prayer, when Scripture mentions prayer, nine out of ten times it is in the context of corporate prayer—people praying together—not individuals praying alone. Our individualistic western church culture has taken the admonition about praying in secret out of context (Matt. 6:6), and made it the motto and standard for our prayer life.

Fortunately, there are some great corporate prayer traditions outside of North America. We need to learn from them. When I preached in churches in the West Indies, I knew that for an hour or more before the Sunday morning service began, most of the congregation had already begun praying together for special needs, for friends and relatives, and for the service that day. South Korean church congregations are well known for coming together to pray for hours before dawn.

4. Traditionally, we focus a lot on *teaching* but little on *training*. In Sunday schools, in sermons, and in home Bible study groups, we focus on teaching—feeding minds and passing on knowledge. What we should be doing is focusing on training—changing lives and growing in holiness. Sadly, books on prophecy are best sellers, not because reading them makes Christians become more like Jesus, give sacrificially to missions, or live more disciplined lives, but because they feed the mind and stimulate the imagination.

This Sunday, we celebrate the start of Holy Week, the most eventful week in the life of Jesus and his disciples. All the happiness surrounding Palm Sunday, however, is no more than the pale light of early dawn in comparison with Resurrection Sunday—when the sun bursts blazing over the horizon.

Jesus rising alive from the tomb! Now *that* is a life-changing event! An event the apostles talked about every day for the rest of their lives. They made it a personal habit and a church tradition.

As should we.

*David Katski. "Palm Sunday." Share Faith.

http://www.faithclipart.com/guide/Christian-Holidays/what-is-palm-sunday.html

⁀ COLUMN 16 ⁀
CELEBRATING GOD'S COSMIC JOKE

The fun started during my first year in Bible school when a number of elements came together and cried out for action.

Consider these essential components:

Prophecy was a major focus in my alma mater, with daily chapel reminders of the imminent return of Christ to rapture the Church. We sang of the trumpet of the Lord and imagined rising to meet the Lord in the air.

My roommate owned one of the first portable reel-to-reel tape players produced. He had a collection of great music, including a recording of a bugle call reveille. I knew where the school's portable loud speaker equipment was stored and how to operate it. My daily chore was to scrub pots and pans in the boiler room, through which one could pass from the basement of the men's dormitory to the basement of the ladies' dormitory.

It was fated that one early morning, all these elements achieved critical mass as my roommate and I carried his equipment through the boiler room, positioned the loud speaker at the bottom of the stairs leading to the girls' dormitory, and hooked up the cables.

Five minutes before the dormitory wake-up buzzer sounded, I turned up the volume to maximum and pushed the play button.

Ta-ta-ta-ta-TAAAA-ta!!!! The Trumpet of the Lord sounded!

It took a full fifteen seconds before we heard the sound of bare feet hitting the floor as the girls jumped out of bed. When we heard feet running towards the stairs, we yanked the cables, grabbed our equipment, and shot back through the boiler room. We stowed the loudspeaker equipment back into its closet and were back in our room when the wake-up buzzer sounded.

At the breakfast tables, the girls excitedly told their stories:

"I jarred awake and thought the Rapture was happening."

"I wondered when I would start rising into the air."

"I ran into the hall and saw others running about, and I was so relieved to see I was not the only one left behind!"

The apostle Paul called the event of the second coming of Jesus a *mystery*, and so was our highly successful prank. It would have remained a mystery if my roommate and I had not succumbed to the temptation to get some credit and modestly allowed the information that we were the culprits to slip out. The staff discipline committee convened and immediately expelled me. No wait, that was in my second year, and for something else—another story. Simulating the Rapture was risky and earned us some demerits, but it was fun.

Have you ever noticed that even little kids love having fun? My grandkids sure do. For most of my youngest grandson's ten years, if he wasn't having fun, he was out finding some. That is still his policy. Jesus, whom His enemies accused of being a "party animal," understands and approves of my grandson's policy. He was emphatic when he proclaimed, "I'm telling you, once and for all, that unless you return to square one and start over like children, you're not even going to get a look at the kingdom, let alone get in" (Matt. 18:3, *The Message*).

In addition to children and college students, other kinds of people are also free of inhibitions and full of fun. People under the influence of a moderate amount of alcohol tend to feel high and have a good time—so are people who are under the influence of the Holy Spirit. The apostle Paul's counsel is to be under the influence of the Spirit because there is no danger of the excess and debauchery that results from drinking too much wine (Eph. 5:18). You can't overdose on the Spirit of God.

Paul often connects God's Spirit with joy. In the midst of a serious explanation about the Jewish people's inability to understand the Good News, he throws in an aside: "Where the Spirit of the Lord is, there is freedom" (2 Cor. 3:17, NIV).

The term "freedom" comes from the Greek term, *eleutheria*, which refers to God's people being free to enjoy living the way God wants them to live. Some scholars say it also carries the meaning of "being released from inhibition and constraint to enjoy pleasure." In other words, Paul says, "Where the Spirit of the Lord is, there is good, clean fun." I am not a Greek expert, and this interpretation is debateable, but it seems to fit in with Paul's comment on being drunk on the Spirit, doesn't it?

Christians have a lot to be happy about. The resurrection of Jesus Christ was the most deliriously joyful event in the history of the world. It still is. It proved without a doubt that He is God and victorious over death, hell, Satan, and all his forces of evil. That is why some denominations celebrate the Sunday after Easter as Holy Hilarity Sunday. It comes from the ancient tradition of celebrating *Risus Paschalis*—God's Holy Joke, the Easter laugh.

Things had been going Satan's way right up to the moment that Jesus' mutilated corpse rose to glorious life again. On Easter morning, God suddenly turned the tables and revealed that Satan had played into God's hands.

What a horrifying surprise! Satan and his forces suddenly realised they were defeated. No doubt they smacked their infernal foreheads and screamed in rage, "If only we had known!" But they hadn't. God in His wisdom had kept His age-old plan of redemption hidden from Satan. Paul says, "If they had known, they would not have crucified the Lord of Glory" (1 Cor. 2:8, NIV).

Unfortunately, April Fool's pranks are about the only thing left of this post-Easter celebration of God's Cosmic Joke on Satan. Too bad. On the Sunday following Easter, wouldn't it be great if all around the world, hundreds of thousands of church services resounded with waves of laughter at the pastors' happy stories, and congregations sang every glad, joyful, and cheerful song in their repertoire?

Maybe fun-loving little kids should organize these church services—or first year Bible college students with an overdeveloped sense of humour.

BROTHER DOG AND SISTER CAT

Earth Day, observed on April 22, provokes the media to expound on pro-environment hype and lamentations about global warming.* Concern about global warming is a hard sell where I live, when the ice is still a meter thick on the lake in front of our house, and half metre-high drifts of snow still cover the lawn.

But, as a responsible citizen and a Christian, I will now do my part to help preserve and improve planet Earth. As I am writing this column, I hear a couple of dogs barking in the neighbour's yard. Good subject. Do North America's dogs and cats contribute to environmental pollution? Hmm? I stepped in some the other day and am beginning to get some thoughts.

How much excrement do they produce? A bit of research on the Internet and a few moments with my calculator indicates that five thousand dogs and cats produce enough feces every day to fill a dumpster. With 150 million dogs and cats living and excreting in North America, that works out to thirty thousand dumpsters loaded with doggie doo and kitty scat. Every day! All that stinky stuff rotting in thousands of landfills, on a million lawns and along miles of gutters all across the continent! How much ozone destroying greenhouse gas does this produce? Should something be done about this situation? These thought-provoking questions are my contribution to Earth Day.

The same news report that alerted me to the upcoming Earth Day also informed me that seventy-seven million children aged six to ten living on planet Earth have no school, no teacher, no books, and no chance of getting any kind of education.** None. They live in Africa, Asia, and South America, in places devastated and ravaged by natural calamities, war, and other man-made disasters. Only token funding is available for the basic education these children need. This bothers me far more than doggie doo, even when it is on my shoe.

While I was thinking of those millions of desperately poor children, made in the image of God, but without a hope for any sort of education, I came across an article from *Lawyers Weekly USA*, stating that the average amount of money left in pet trusts is $25,000.*** Pet trusts? Yes, North Americans are putting brother dog or sister cat in their will, setting up trusts to take care of their pets after they die.

This led me to check a pet adopting website that helpfully provided a budget for the new owner. Not including the purchase price, it costs about $600 per year to own and care for a cat or medium-sized dog.****

The Save the Children organization that produced the report on the seventy-seven million children without schools, calculates about $9 billion is needed to provide primary education for them.** Hmm?

Based on the percentage of Christians in the total population, possibly about fifteen million cats and dogs are owned by Christians in North America. That got me dreaming.

Let's say we Christians keep track of how much we spend on our cat, dog, or other companion pet each year, and then give that same amount of money, over and above our regular giving, to meet some humanitarian need. At a low average of $600 per pet, that would be $9 billion, just the amount needed to provide basic education for seventy-seven million learning deprived children.

I just now offered a prayer of profound thanks to God for my own education and that of my children, grandchildren, and other kids in my society. We are not deprived, and we need to be thankful. But that's not enough.

I can still see that huge crowd of little school-age boys and girls, twice the entire population of Canada, without schools or teachers. All those kids, made in the image of God, but walking on in ignorance into a dark future!

I don't own a pet, but I'm reaching for my chequebook anyway. I need to brighten the future for at least a few of those unschooled kids.

It just started snowing again, heavily. Happy Earth Day!

*"Earth Day." Earth Day Network. http://www.earthday.net

**"Canada Urged to Help Millions Denied School in War-Torn Nations." CBS News. 2010. http://www.cbc.ca/canada/story/2007/04/16/children-education.html

***"Animal Owners Set up Trust Funds for Their Pets." USA Today. 2008. http://www.usatoday.com/news/nation/2002-08-15-pettrust_x.htm

****"The Cost of Owning a Dog." Raising Spot.com. 2010. http://www.raisingspot.com/adopting/cost_of_owning_dog.php

MUCH MORE THAN HAULING STUFF

"How much longer, Daddy?" Valorie, our five-year-old daughter, had been asking all day. Now she added, "My knee is really hurting."

"I think we'll get there before dark," I said, hoping there would be no more breakdowns. My wife, Jo, and our two younger daughters, Leanne and Cheryl, also looked relieved to hear the end was near. For four days, we had endured an agonizing, bone-jarring ride to a Canela village to start our Bible translation ministry. No wonder the rheumatoid arthritis in Valorie's knee was flaring up.

The Canela village lay only fifty miles south of the nearest town, but it took days to grind through sand, mud, and Brazilian bush to get around the headwaters of a deep, swift-flowing river.

Naturally we worked to prepare an airstrip during our first few months in the village. The Canelas chopped down trees and dug out stumps, excited about the "metal bird" coming to their village. They also crowded around our two-way, shortwave radio to listen in fascination to our daily radio contacts with the mission centre four hundred miles away.

Capi, our Canela neighbour, often explained our radio to sceptical visitors from another Canela village. "Yes. He talks into that little black box on the end of that curly vine. His talk goes up to that long metal vine between those two poles. Then it flies through the air all the way to the big city. He can even talk to airplanes."

Village bystanders would nod their heads and say, "True, true."

The day the first plane was to land, dozens of excited villagers crowded near, trying to understand the Portuguese squawking from the radio as Paul, the pilot, reported his progress to the radio operator on the mission centre in the city.

Finally the radio crackled a location they all recognized—the name of the town fifty miles from the village. "The plane will be here soon," I told the growing and increasingly more animated group of Canelas.

Time was up. But scanning the northern horizon, we saw nothing. Just then the radio squawked again, "Jack, I should be close, but I can't see your village."

"There it is!" one sharp-eyed teenager yelled, pointing to a speck low on the eastern horizon.

"We can see you, Paul," I said into the mike. "Turn and fly towards sunset."

"Okay, Jack, I'm turning now."

The villagers all listened intently, most of them understanding this exchange.

Then, as the JAARS Helio Courier banked and flew directly towards us, I heard a great gasp from the group, and they all began to talk at once.

"Look! It's turning just as he said."

"It's coming this way!"

"He really can send his talk on that vine!"

The most surprised was my voluble neighbour, Capi. Yes, the very one who had so eloquently tried to convince dubious visitors that I could talk to airplanes.

Before that first plane even landed, God had already used the event to show the Canela people that they could believe us. We were not like the traders who lied to them about the price of goods and made promises they never kept. No matter how fantastic our stories, or how great our promises, Canelas were learning they could believe us to tell the truth—every time. What a foundation on which to build a Bible translation ministry! We had a very hard-to-believe Story to tell them.

For twenty-two years, a succession of pilots—Paul, Skip, Chuck, Mike, Don, Fritz, Hal, and Neil—made repeated trips to the Canela village. They took our daughters to boarding school, delivered books, mail, and medicines, and returned Canela translation helpers to the village after workshops in the city.

The plane was invaluable in maintaining good relationships with the government; bringing in officials who needed to see a field linguistic and literacy project first-hand; or anthropologists, researchers, doctors, and others who checked out the Canelas' basic needs for medical aid, hygiene, and clean water. These visitors were often surprised at how much we provided through the plane service.

The pilots never flew an empty airplane. Several times the plane arrived full of little things—hundreds of day-old, purebred chicks to improve the inbred local chicken population. Soon village chickens were larger and healthier than the Canelas had ever seen.

One time the plane was the hearse carrying home the body of Jaco, our best translation helper and the first believer, who died in the hospital following complications from an operation. It was the pilot who comforted and calmed the widow on the four-hour flight as she sobbed in the seat beside him.

In August 1990, the plane made its last essential flights for the Canela translation program. Fittingly, it brought my elderly parents and Jo's mom to the Canela village to participate in the dedication and first distribution of the Canela partial Bible. Our parents remembered the decades-long pain of separation from us and their grandchildren. But as they saw scores of believers, mostly young men and women, receive their copy of the Bible in Canela, they said to each other, "It cost us, but it was worth it."

JAARS pilots and their airplanes had a major impact on the Canelas and the Bible translation program, far beyond hauling us with our stuff to and from the village. How much longer would it have taken to complete our translation program without dedicated pilots and their aircraft?

Sometimes I wonder, would we have been able to do it at all?

GOD THE FUNDRAISER

My mind often buzzes with thoughts about fundraising. Not surprising since twice a year I travel five weeks to twenty-five cities challenging audiences to get involved in Bible translation through prayer, volunteer work, and especially financial support. Much of the time, I feel like Moses urging the people to volunteer their skills to build the tabernacle and to give gold, silver, bronze, and other precious materials (Exod. 35).

Money for missions is a vitally important subject, yet God's people dislike talking about it. Some years ago, I heard Dr. Luis Palau, internationally known evangelist and world mission leader, say something I had never before heard in church. I sat in the front row of the huge church and cheered silently as he urged young people to consider cross-cultural missions as a career. Then he stepped away from the pulpit and focused on the hundreds of young people sitting in a reserved area near the front.

"Young people," he said. "If you think you can do something great for God in the world of missions without learning to raise funds, you will be bitterly disappointed. You cannot live or work without money, and you must accept the fact that you, yourself, will be the person to raise the largest part of it."

Missionaries are lifelong fundraisers, and some of us take a lifetime to learn how. When Jo and I joined Wycliffe over forty-five years ago, we knew we would not get a guaranteed income. We accepted the policy requiring us to raise all the money for our personal and ministry expenses from our family, friends, and church.

We also accepted some fundraising advice that was quite popular in the Christian sub-culture at that time and often used by God to supply the needs of missionaries.

"Just pray for God to supply your needs," our Wycliffe mentors told us. "Tell people all about your ministry, but, unless they specifically ask you, don't tell anyone that you need money or how much you need. And most of all, never ask anyone to give you money."

That is like telling Billy Graham, "Just pray for God to save people. Tell them all about how great it is to be a child of God, but, unless they specifically ask you, don't tell anyone how to become one. And most of all, never invite anyone to be saved." The comparison is apt since both fundraisers and evangelists invite people to take a step of faith.

Jo and I followed that time-honoured advice for seven poverty-stricken years. It was not until we adopted a biblical alternative to the traditional method of raising funds that our income started to rise to meet our personal and ministry needs.

First, we followed King David's biblical example of fundraising to build the temple (1 Chron. 29). David first gave massive amounts of his own personal treasure (v. 2-3), and then asked others to give themselves, their skills, and their treasure (v. 5). Underlying this was the understanding that God owned everything, that He is the source of all wealth, and people are simply His money managers (v. 10-12).

Secondly, Jo and I recognized several levels of motivation to raise funds. We wanted money for our Bible translation ministry. We also wanted God to bless generously those who gave generously. But our highest motivation was that God would be worshipped more. Jo and I would worship God and thank Him for the financial provision to serve Him better. Our financial partners would worship God and thank Him for His blessings. The people who benefitted from our ministry, the Canelas, would worship Him as their newfound Lord and Saviour.

Thirdly, we recognized that just as the Holy Spirit is the great Soulwinner, drawing people to Himself, He is also the great Fundraiser, moving people to give to His work. Moses and David both asked for and received gifts from people whose hearts the great Fundraiser had touched and had made willing to give.

Jo and I started using a *personal evangelism* model of fundraising: We did *not* simply pray for God to supply all our needs, although that is exactly what He ended up doing.

Instead we prayed:

Send your Holy Spirit to prepare the hearts of people to give to Your work.

Bring us into contact with people whose hearts You have prepared and give us opportunity to share the vision of the ministry among the Canela You have given us.

Give us opportunities to invite prepared and informed people to be financial partners with us in our ministry.

Help them to respond to our invitation to partner with us and join our support team.

As we prayed these four prayers, we became more aware of God leading us to develop relationships with people and to minister to them. As the Holy Spirit prepared willing hearts, our inviting people to partner with us became natural and smooth, not forced and awkward.

We now see ourselves not as poor, needy missionaries desperately looking for a handout, but as Moses and David, fully given over to the task of ministry. Like them, we confidently ask God's people, whose hearts He has already prepared, to give to His work.

God, the real Fundraiser, works within the givers' hearts. We simply invite them to give in to God's urging. It is not complicated or manipulative.

Fundraising, like evangelism, is a miracle—a miracle of faith.

✦ Column 20 ✦
We Blame Our Mothers, and Rightly So

One day, when I was about seven years old, my mama asked me what I would like to be when I grew up. I responded, *"Mischien wel een zendeling"* —"Maybe a missionary." Where did I get that idea at such a young age? From my mother, of course. Aren't mothers to blame for everything in our lives?

I remember learning to write, but I cannot remember a time that I didn't know how to read. My mama was responsible. As the young mother of a toddler, she read to me daily from the *Kinderbijbel*, the Children's Bible, and prayed with me. I practically memorized those illustrated stories as I sat on her lap and studied the sensibly spelled Dutch words on the page. Before I started school, she gave me books from the children's library to read. Many of them were short stories of missionaries serving in Indonesia, a Dutch colony at that time. I can still remember some of those stories today, more than six decades later.

My mother knew that the two most impactful influences in our lives are the people we interact with and the books we read. She had little power over which kids I played with in the street or in the school playground, but she did have control over what books I read. It is her fault that I became a lifelong reader.

She was always in favour of me becoming a missionary. Even on the day Jo and I left for Brazil, taking her only grandchildren away from her for four years, she blessed us, despite the heavy emotional price she paid. Later, when she was nearly sixty years old, she further proved her missions passion when she accompanied my dad to Brazil to work together for three months building a house for our family on the missions centre in Belem. She did what she could in practical ways, sewing curtains, painting, and cleaning up the job site. Yes, my mother is responsible for me becoming a missionary.

Jo's mother was also responsible for her becoming a missionary, though in a much less overt way. When Jo was only a baby, her mom quietly prayed and dedicated her to God, praying she would be a missionary. She continued to pray for Jo and was happy when she decided to go to Bible school. She encouraged her and prayed for her all those years.

Very wisely, she never told Jo that she had dedicated her as a baby to be a missionary. She didn't want Jo to feel that pressure. It was not until after Jo had graduated from Bible school twenty-two years later, and was preparing to leave for Biola University to take a course in missionary medicine, that her mom finally told her. Jo's mom definitely was the culprit, fully responsible, under God, for making her a missionary.

Both Jo's mom and mine traveled to the Canela village in August of 1990 to participate in the final dedication and distribution of the partial Bible in Canela. Speaking for both of them, Jo's mom said, "It was hard to be separated from our kids, but seeing the Canelas receive God's Word makes us realize it was worth it."

Our three daughters can also blame their mom for many things in their lives. Jo influenced our daughters through prayer just like her mom and mine did. She also helped me develop a system whereby we paid our teenage daughters to read the kinds of books we wanted them to read. Beyond prayer and books, she also taught them life skills like sewing, cooking, and baking. Open house gatherings at the Popjes place on Belem centre were famous for plenty of goodies, prepared by Jo and the girls. No wonder that today our daughters are avid readers who love cooking and baking and preparing gourmet foods. And, of course, they are very much in favour of cross-cultural foreign missions.

Our three daughters are mothers to our eight grandchildren. They continue the tradition of influencing them to love God deeply, to pray fervently, to read copiously, and to be involved in missions. Leanne's two eighteen year-old boys have built houses in Mexico and have been on two school-sponsored, ten-day missions trips to Guatemala. Valorie's four girls have accompanied their parents on short missions trips to Mexico, Pakistan, and Thailand. Cheryl's two children are looking forward to their turn to go on a missions trip.

In the summer of 2009, our family of fifteen traveled to Brazil for a six-week trip. The first place we visited was Belem where we used to live on the missions centre and where our daughters went to school. Then, after a nineteen-year absence, we visited the Canela village where we worked as linguist-Bible translators for twenty-two years. The Canelas were delighted to see us, and we were overjoyed to be there. Our eight grandchildren finally saw for themselves the people and village they had heard so much about. During the last weeks, we toured some of the places for which Brazil is famous. It was a once-in-lifetime experience!

Who thought up this idea and made most of the arrangements? Jo, Valorie, Leanne, and Cheryl—the mothers, of course.

Whom else would we blame?

→ COLUMN 21 ←
OF RATS AND CHRISTIANS

Canada's national news magazine, *Maclean's*, at times assumes a biblical prophetic ministry rivalling the critical thunderings of the prophet Isaiah thousands of years ago.

One front-page article headlined, *Lawyers are Rats*, was based on an exclusive interview with a veteran Canadian lawyer who wrote a book calling the legal profession to account. He described lawyers as "amoral, obsessed with making money, rife with fraudulent and unethical activity, indifferent to issues of justice, and poorly regulated."*

You can imagine the furious letters from lawyers demanding an apology that filled the expanded *Letters from Readers* section in the next issue. They claimed that only a few lawyers would fit this negative description.

The editors, however, stood their ground. They quoted numerous legal experts, some of them highly placed justices, who for years have spoken publicly and written about the "lack of ethics" and the "crisis of professionalism" among lawyers.

The key problem is that lawyers are supposed to police themselves and each other, but fail to do so. Lawyers admit that some of their colleagues are "rats," but still allow them to continue their unethical behaviour—*this* is where the problem lies.

Lawyers, of course, are not the only professionals who fit this profile. Doctors are also notoriously easy on their colleagues caught in unprofessional behaviour. A national medical legal overseer wrote, "The rap on physicians is that they are loath to turn in one of their colleagues, and the record seems to suggest that there is truth to this allegation."** Ethics are overlooked in other areas of medicine, too. Pharmaceutical research scientists are routinely in gross conflict of interest with the drug industry.

Unfortunately, the Christian Church is also guilty of failing to police Herself. We are swamped with stories about priests pleading guilty to child sexual abuse and pastors who are sexual predators. Instead of calling them to account, the priests' bishops often simply move the abusers from one church to another where, after some time, they make new victims. When caught, the predatory pastors are fired from their position, but often allowed to move to another city and start their sinful lifestyle all over again.

Nor is it just church leaders who live immorally or behave unethically. We ordinary folk in the pew are just as guilty. The problem is, just as with the lawyers, the doctors, and the church leaders, no one holds us personally accountable. When we try to live a clean life by ourselves, we fail.

We cannot do it. Here's why: God did not design human beings to live well in isolation from each other.

As recorded in the first chapter of Genesis, each time that God created something new, He looked at it, was pleased, and said, "This is good." In chapter two, however, He created Adam, looked at him, was *not* pleased, and said, "It is *not* good for man to be alone," and immediately made another human being to be with Adam.

God designed us to live in families and interact with people in close, caring communities. Each local church should be a place where people can be honest, open, and transparent and receive the encouragement, correction, and help they need to live right.

Each church needs someone outside its local membership that will hold it accountable to biblical standards. Each church leader needs to have someone to whom he or she is accountable. Each family leader needs to have someone from outside the family who can ask him or her the hard questions. So does every individual Christian.

Sometimes people tell me, "Our church elders' board is accountable to God and Him alone," or "I am accountable to God alone for how I lead my family or live my life." They are right. Someday, we will each give account to God Himself. But, until then, God knows that ordinary human beings, just like medical and legal professionals, tend to fail at policing themselves. Christians find it difficult to be accountable to an invisible Spirit. God designed us to need another human being to help us live right—someone to look us in the eye and hold us accountable for the way we live.

Many years ago, when I was about to take on a challenging, high profile leadership role, I thought deeply about the classic temptations of power, sex, and money. Then I wrote out seven questions that I hoped no one would ever ask me. I sealed these questions in an envelope and gave them to a trusted friend.

"Please come into my office," I said, "look me in the eye and ask me these questions at least once a week."

His weekly sessions were a powerful aid for me in living a clean life. The list has now grown to twelve questions, and I still have someone who asks me the questions—including the last one, "Have you just lied to me about any of the previous questions?"

Lawyers are rats. So are we all. We need all the help we can get to live the way God wants us to live, not like rats but like loving human beings.

Jesus summarized God's two greatest commands to human beings: "'Hear, O Israel, the Lord our God, the Lord is one. Love the Lord your God with all your heart and with all your soul and with all your mind and with all your strength.' The second is this: 'Love your neighbour as yourself'" (Mark 12:29-31, NIV).

None of us can fully attain that standard in our own strength. God designed us to operate with other people around us to help us by holding us accountable. We ignore His design at our peril.

*"Lawyers are Rats Interview." Lawyer Philip Slayton talks to Kate Fillion. *Maclean's*. 6 August 2007.

**Michael Scott. "Reflections on Ethics Self-Policing." *Governmental and Legal Affairs*. December 2004. http://www.asahq.org/Newsletters/2004/12_04/scott.html#scott

PRIMING OUR BEHAVIOUR

So there I was, lying in my hammock, sipping a cold drink and enjoying some light summer reading in the *Journal of Personality and Social Psychology*. The article, "Automaticity of Social Behaviour: Direct Effects of Trait Construct and Stereotype Activation on Action" caught my eye. "This would make a good *Look* article," I thought.

(Okay, I confess, although the hammock and cold drink part are true, I didn't read the whole article—only a few quotes from it. And I read them in another, much more easy-to-read book called *Blink* by Malcolm Gladwell.*)

While reading, I remembered living on a farm as a twelve-year old. My daily chore was to pump and haul water. I always took along a can of clean water to pour into the top of the pump before working the handle that brought up the water to fill my pails. Priming the pump softened and swelled the leather disk valves and increased the pump's lifting power. Nowadays, I prime my lawnmower by pushing the rubber bulb to pump a bit of gas into the cylinder. It won't start if I don't.

It appears that we human beings also operate in response to priming. In fact, the way we are primed influences our behaviour. The article told how researchers staged an experiment using a number of undergraduates as subjects. They gave every student one of two sets of exercises in which they had to unscramble a set of mixed up sentences.

Sprinkled throughout one set of exercises were words like "aggressive," "bold," "rude," "bother," "disturb," "intrude," and "infringe." The other set had a few words like "respect," "considerate," "appreciate," "patient," "yield," "polite," and "courteous." The key words were so few in each exercise set that the students never caught on to what was going on.

After completing the unscrambling exercise, the students followed instructions to walk down the hall to another office to ask the person running the experiment about their next assignment.

Whenever a student arrived at the office, however, the researcher was always busy, locked in conversation with someone else—a confederate who was standing in the hallway, blocking the doorway to the office. The object of the experiment was to see if the students who were primed with polite words would take longer to interrupt the conversation than those primed with rude words. He had a stopwatch ready to check the difference—if any.

He need not have bothered with the stopwatch. All the people who were unconsciously primed with rude words eventually interrupted, some almost immediately, others after five or six minutes. On the other hand, nine out of ten students primed with polite words never interrupted at all, patiently waiting the full ten minutes when the experiment was stopped.

In another experiment, two other researchers randomly divided a large number of students into two groups. They instructed one group to list as many characteristics of university professors as they could in five minutes. They assigned the other group to list the characteristics of violently disruptive soccer fans. They then asked each student forty-two fairly difficult questions from the board game Trivial Pursuit. The ones who had been primed to think about soccer hooligans got 42 percent right, while those who had been thinking about university professors got 55 percent right.

The "professor" group did not know more than the "violent soccer fan" group. They were not smarter, or more focused, or more serious. They had simply been primed to think smart—13 percent smarter than the other group. That can be the difference between success and failure.

God designed us human beings to operate best when we are primed with positive thoughts—biblical truth. Thousands of years ago wise King Solomon observed, "As a man thinketh in his heart, so is he" (Prov. 23:7, KJV). God made us in His own image. God is love. God is truth. He is primed to operate consistently in ultimate love and truth. That is how He wants us to be primed.

If we want to function to the best of our ability during the day, we need to stop priming ourselves with negative things like angry arguments at breakfast or the early morning newscast, which mostly focuses on the work of Satan.

Instead, we need to take the apostle Paul's advice, who two thousand years ago, told the Christians in Philippi to prime themselves with positive thoughts. ". . . you'll do best by filling your minds and meditating on things true, noble, reputable, authentic, compelling, gracious—the best, not the worst; the beautiful, not the ugly; things to praise, not things to curse" (Phil. 4:8, *The Message*).

I feel bad for people who habitually prime themselves with negative, depressing, ugly, and false thoughts. Some of us constantly set ourselves up for negative attitudes and behaviour through our critical conversations, the material we read, the music lyrics we listen to, or the videos we watch.

I feel even worse for the billions of people who know nothing of the Bible, an ancient book thousands of years ahead of current psychological research, and packed with beautiful, positive, and truth-oriented thoughts. Among them are hundreds of millions of people who speak languages in which no part of the Bible has yet been translated.

Without God's Word in their language, how can these people prime themselves with positive truth so that they can live to the utmost of their capacity? How can they live in fullness of joy, in unchanging truth, and to their personal best? How can they live in the way God, their Creator, intended for them to live—exhibiting His image?

*Malcolm Gladwell, *Blink: The Power of Thinking Without Thinking* (New York: Time Warner Book Group, 2005).

THE SKIN OF A HOLE

"Do you have a *krehkah* you can give me?" a Canela village friend asked me one morning.

"A what?" I responded. He repeated his question.

"What on earth is a *krehkah*?" I wondered. I knew the word *kah* meant "skin," as in *pohkah* meaning "skin of a deer." But *krehkah*? A *kreh* is any kind of hole: in the ground, in a tree, even in a piece of cloth. So *krehkah* would be "hole-skin." What is the skin of a hole? It didn't make sense.

My friend solved the mystery as he reached past the stack of books and cans of Spam I had just unpacked and picked up the empty cardboard box. "This *krehkah* is just the right size for what I need," he said.

I finally got it. A box is a hole with a cardboard skin around it. Therefore, it is the skin of a hole, or a hole-skin. Simple once you catch on. I learned that the Canelas use the term to indicate any kind of box, suitcase, or stiff sided basket.

I think of that word when I read the prophet Habakkuk's description of idols (2:19). The outsides of the idol images are gold and silver, beautifully dressed and decorated with jewels. They look fabulous, but there is nothing alive inside, merely dead wood or stone. The idols are just *hole-skins*, with nothing of God or spiritual life inside.

Just like the gilded idols of Habakkuk's time, our idols today are also only beautiful hole-skins. We too tend to replace God with things that look great on the outside but are spiritually empty.

Anne Graham Lotz, in her little booklet *My Jesus is Everything*, poetically lists a number of activities that often take God's place:

Sports, sex, success
Honours, health, hobbies

Career, clubs, children, church
Finances, family, friends, fame, fortune
Pleasure, popularity, position, possessions, politics, power, prestige*

As Christians, many of us get enormous satisfaction from being involved in church activities. We love the fellowship and Bible studies with other Christians, serving in choirs and on worship music teams, and going on mission trips. Some of us get deeply involved in specialty ministries or ride religious hobbyhorses—everything from prophecy to politics, from environmentalism to anti-abortion, and yes, even Bible translation. As satisfying and important as these are, they are merely beautiful idols—unless God is at the centre of each of them.

Each of us has to ask ourselves some questions and be brutally honest in answering them.

Never mind all the things I do, am I becoming more like Jesus?

Are my relationships with Him and with His people growing deeper and stronger?

Is my character clean and pure, my life without secrets?

Do I live aware that Jesus, through the Holy Spirit, is alive in me?

Unless I can answer "Yes" to these questions, all my activities are merely the beautiful skin of a hole.

It is so easy to count our actions and accomplishments. They are there for everyone to see and admire. People ask me, "At how many events do you speak each year?" I tell them, and they are suitably impressed—the same with the number of columns, articles, and books I write. But that is all outside activity. They could simply be admiring the jewels on Jack's ministry idol.

We need to answer the important question, "Is there spiritual life inside?" As a follower of Jesus, I am His representative on earth. I am supposed to embody Him. I should be seeing the way He sees.

When Jesus saw the crowds, he felt sorry for them. They seemed like sheep without a shepherd, and He met their needs. I speak at many banquets each year and always tell this story as an illustration. But when I see the crowds of banquet guests, do I see them as Jesus sees them—as precious souls for which he died, people with deep personal needs? Or do I see them merely as potential volunteers and donors for the mission projects we are promoting, or as prospective customers to buy my books?

If I do not see these people with the eyes of Jesus, my ministry is merely a *krehkah*, a skin around a whole lot of nothing.

But when you and I are aware—moment by moment—that Jesus lives within, there is no limit to what He can do in our lives.

---

*Anne Graham Lotz. *My Jesus Is...Everything!* (Thomas Nelson, 2005).

Papa's Cigars, Mama's Violets, and God's Love

Fathers teach—mostly by example. My father's example put a strong desire in my eleven-year-old heart to be a cigar smoker like he was. Loving fathers also teach their children by exposing them to experiences that teach. My father, or *Papa* as I called him, was a loving father.

He exemplified the Dutch saying, *Hij is geen man die niet roken kan.* "A man who can't smoke is not a real man. " For years, I had envied my *Papa*, my *Opa* 'grandpa', and all my uncles who often smoked cigars on Sunday as they walked home from church. Sometimes they had a second cigar with coffee while lunch was being prepared. I couldn't wait until I was a teenager and could be a real man.

I couldn't wait, and I didn't. I saved the pennies and nickels I earned as tips when delivering orders to customers of *Papa's* store. One day I walked into the tobacco shop where *Papa* often sent me to buy cigars for him and, laying my money on the counter, asked if it was enough to buy a cigar. It was!

When I got home, I realized I had not thought through my plan too well. I could not hide the cigar in the house because my Mama would be sure to find it when cleaning house, which she was always doing. So I hid my carefully wrapped package outside, behind the drain spout along the wall. It was dry—the spider webs testified to that—and totally safe from prying parental eyes.

But it wasn't safe from the eyes of the Saturday afternoon hired gardener! He turned my cigar over to *Mama* who passed it on to *Papa* who confronted me with it after supper. To my surprise and relief, he was not angry but simply said, "So you want to smoke a cigar. Fine, we'll smoke our cigars together after church tomorrow." Wow! I was beginning to feel like a real man already!

Arriving home from church the next day, he picked out a cigar for himself, clipped the end and lit it. I unwrapped my cigar, clipped the end and lit it. Then we walked out the front door puffing contentedly—in between my coughing spells. As we sauntered around the block, I started to get the hang of it and inhaled deeply from time to time.

All was well, and I felt my real manhood arriving several years early, but half way around the block I stumbled—the sidewalk seemed to be moving. I walked along, not saying much, while *Papa* kept saying, "Come on, take another puff, your cigar is going out." I was sort of hoping it would. By the time the house was in view I was sweating, my stomach hurt, and, when we finally got to our gate, all I could do was lean over the fence and vomit onto *Mama's* violets.

Yes, *Papa* was a great teacher. I never started smoking. Seven years later, after smoking for thirty years, he strove for a full year to quit. As I watched his struggle, he taught me another lesson. Smoking cigars together and allowing me to feel deathly ill was his way of showing love to his oldest son.

God, our Heavenly Father, is also a loving Father. He teaches us by example—to live and do, think and say, and act and work, just as He does. To be godly means to be God-like. Like God, we need to love people, forgive, and be merciful, patient, and kind—all those wonderful character traits we see in Jesus, His Son.

Just like my *Papa*, God also exposes us to experiences that teach us. He allows us to live through the consequences of our actions, even when our actions result in nasty, unpleasant things like illnesses or accidents, fines or firings, and painful, broken relationships. Sometimes He provides negative experiences that are not of our own making: computer crashes, economic meltdowns, loss of jobs, or loss through sickness, accident, fire, or robbery.

How do we handle these pains and problems? By remembering that God loves us, in spite of what it feels like at the moment. It took seven years before I understood fully that when my *Papa* took me on that cigar smoking walk, it was for my ultimate good. It might take seven years for us to understand that God's action was for our ultimate good. We may not know until we leave time and enter eternity. In the meantime, we believe that He loves us and that He is good, all the time.

So what does this have to do with missions and Bible translation?

Several billion people live thinking that there is neither rhyme nor reason to the cosmos. Everything happens by chance, or is the result of blind, unpredictable fate. Another billion live thinking that everything is foreordained and will happen no matter what they do. And it may not be good for them. These people badly need to hear the message that God is in charge, that He is good, and that He loves them.

Then there is a minority of 200 million—about six times the population of Canada—who have absolutely no chance of hearing the message of God's love since it has never been translated into their languages.

That makes me feel sick—even sicker than I was on that Sunday I leaned over the fence and . . . !

THE DAY DADDY BLEW IT

The day I blew it as a father and learned an important lesson from my oldest daughter started much like any other Tuesday—the day reserved for making pastoral visits to our parishioners.

I dressed our two-year-old Valorie in her snowsuit and packed her into the makeshift car seat in the rear of our 1962 Volkswagen Beetle. Jo gathered up her purse and diaper bag and, pregnant with Leanne, struggled into the passenger seat.

I asked Jo to brief me on the first of the families on the list. As she began to remind me of names and relationships, little Valorie kept asking questions:

"Where are we going? When are we going to get there? Will there be kids for me to play with?"

Her constant questions interfered with my executive briefing, and I suddenly turned and brusquely said over my shoulder, "Valorie, I'm getting tired of all those questions. Please sit and be quiet."

For the next few minutes everything was quiet as Jo and I discussed the people we were going to visit, what topics to bring up, and which ones to avoid. Switching lanes I glanced into the rear view mirror and saw Valorie's little face crumpled with grief. Tears were streaming down her cheeks; her little shoulders were heaving with silent sobs.

"What's the matter with Val?" I asked Jo, having already forgotten my exasperated outburst.

As Jo turned to face Val, I heard her little voice sobbing, "Daddy is getting tired of me."

Pow! Oof! Feeling as if I had been punched in the stomach, I pulled over to the curb and, leaning my head on the steering wheel, cried bitterly. We pulled her into the front with us and made a hug sandwich until we all stopped crying.

Jo and I wanted the best for our little girl. I had no intention of hurting her, or making her feel unwanted. We certainly did not want to place our ministry work at a higher priority than raising our child. Yet that is exactly what I had just done.

What's more, according to studies done by professor Eric Knudsen, PhD of *Stanford University School of Medicine*, I had verbally knocked her down to a low priority while she was at the most vulnerable, sensitive, and impressionable age.*

All parents want the best for their kids. We buy them expensive toys, expose them to good music, organize play dates with *nice* kids, and we pick out the best school we can afford. We want them to interact well with others and be successful in whatever they decide to do in their life. We all realize that success in reaching life goals in the future depends a lot on our education today. That is why we especially want our children to do well in school.

Yet, according to Dr. Knudsen and his three fellow members of the *National Scientific Council on the Developing Child*, it is the *earliest* years of life, long before starting school, that forever shape a future-adult's ability to learn. Working independently, the four authors each concluded that a child doing well in school does not depend as much on the quality of an education as on the healthy interactions with parents during the early preschool years.

"It's all about playing with your child," said Dr. Knudsen. "A child's eventual ability to learn calculus or a second language starts with the neurons that are shaped by positive interactions with nurturing adults."

One of the authors of the study, Jack P. Shonkoff, MD, founding director of the newly established *Harvard Center on Children*, said, "The key issue is the nature of kids' relationships with the important people in their lives. It's not about the toys, it's about the human connection."

Not surprisingly, the Bible speaks to this issue as well: "Parents, don't come down too hard on your children or you'll crush their spirits" (Col. 3:21, *The Message*).

I certainly crushed Valorie's spirit that Tuesday in the Volkswagen. Ouch! That painful lesson over forty years ago motivated me to work hard toward having solid, positive relationships with my children.

As Jo and I started the Canela Bible translation program, the temptation to put our ministry before our kids grew exponentially. "Learning the Canela language and translating the Bible into it" was a project that could have consumed several lifetimes. We had to be on guard constantly to put our little ones first—taking time to play with them, appreciate them, have fun with them, and let them know they are important to us.

I am sorry for the pain I caused my little daughter, but I am not sorry for the lesson I learned. Put your kids first. They are your primary ministry. All other work for God is secondary.

*Amy Adams. *"How to Build a Better Brain."* 26 June, 2006. http://www.eurekalert.org/pub_releases/2006-06/sumc-htb062606.php

THE GREAT COLLECTOR

The money collectors are in a panic. Bankers, money managers and government officials have been meeting to try to mitigate the economic problems started by very loose lending practices. Governments are injecting money into the financial systems of their nations to stave off economic collapse.

We keep hearing comparisons with the horrible Great Depression of the 1930s when banks failed in every part of North America, and millions of people were out of work. Hunger and poverty stalked the land.

I am not an economist with a secret solution, but I am not in a panic. I believe that God is still in control and that none of these fiscal developments are a surprise to Him. Even the terrifying stories of the Depression years don't bother me. Here's why:

The Golden Gate Bridge in San Francisco is one of the greatest bridges in the world. Yet it was built in 1934, in the middle of the Depression. During those same Depression years, God moved His people to found or grow dozens of Bible schools throughout North America. In Canada, for instance, my own alma mater, Berean Bible College, grew out of the Prophetic Bible Institute which was started in 1928 and flourished in the 1930s. Peace River Bible Institute was established in 1933. Saskatchewan's Briercrest Bible Institute opened its doors in 1935. During the 1930s, world famous Prairie Bible Institute founded its three general education Christian schools. During that same Depression decade, Prairie Bible Institute built the Prairie Tabernacle which seated forty-three hundred people and was, for decades, Canada's largest religious auditorium.

Evangelical Mission agencies experienced phenomenal growth during the 1930s. What's more, Wycliffe's Cameron Townsend, in that same decade, founded what would become Wycliffe Bible Translators. I can hardly wait to see what great things God is going to do in the next Depression!

Now, back to collectors. Money translates easily into all sorts of things or activities that we need or want, so it's easy to understand what makes collecting money a popular pursuit. But our drive to collect is not limited to money. As a child, I collected stamps. My late mother-in-law had hundreds of sets of salt and pepper shakers. A grandson collects comic books, and my wife used to collect orchids.

When we lived in Brazil, I showed my love for Jo by bringing her orchids for her collection which grew to forty different kinds. Even when I traveled in the jungle without Jo, I would watch for orchids on tree trunks and branches high above the trail. When I spotted an orchid, I would climb up, braving stinging ants, or poke it down with a long pole.

When I got home, I would hand Jo a plastic garbage bag with the latest finds. After a quick welcome home kiss, she would hurry outside to empty the bag on the lawn. Then the fun would start.

"Oh, here is another one of the pretty brown and yellow ones that look like dancing girls. Here is one without blooms, but I think it is one of those big, dark purple, floppy ones!"

But the best was yet to come. "Hey, here's a kind I don't have yet. It's altogether different from any of the others! Oh, thank you, honey!"

I would sit on the step and smilingly watch her tying the new acquisitions to her "orchid tree."

Where does that drive to collect come from? It comes from God. He made us in His image—to be just like Him. According to Malachi 3:17, God collects people who repent, follow, and obey Him. He treats them as His special treasure. God collects men, women and children who respond to Him in faith from every tribe, language, and nation (Rev. 5:9).

Just as my wife was happy to get new additions to her orchid collection, so God rejoices when He adds even one repentant sinner to His collection (Luke 15:7). I can just imagine the scene:

"Oh, look at them all. Red and yellow, black and white. They are so precious. I love them all."

But then comes the best part. "Hey, here's one from a people group I don't have yet. This one is altogether different from any of the others."

Just imagine the celebration in heaven when the first person from a just-reached people group repents. He begins to worship and praise God. The heavenly choirs fall silent as they listen to praise in a language never before heard in heaven. Then they burst out in joyous special celebration as God adds yet another people group to His collection.

I wonder how those choirs will celebrate when the *first* person of the *last* language group turns to God, and God's collection is finally complete (Rev. 7:9)!

I showed Jo that I loved her by bringing her orchids, and she showed me how pleased she was. We show God that we love Him by bringing Him people, and He will show us how pleased He is. Daniel 12:3 gives us some idea: ". . . and those who lead many to righteousness will shine like the stars forever" (NLT).

Thousands of people groups are still missing from God's collection. Every person involved in Bible translation work helps to bring Him new people groups. Everyone, from hands-on translators in the field to prayer partners at home, from computer technicians to financial partners of the Bible translation task—all are focused on completing God's Great Collection.

And, Second Great Depression or not, it will be completed!

THE CANADA DAY GIFT

I did not like being a poor, ignorant immigrant, but I loved being in Canada. Except for leaving dozens of relatives and all our friends, everything about coming to Canada was good: plenty of space, many opportunities, and huge dreams. But Canada's greatest gift to our family arrived within a week or so of Canada Day in 1952.

I had no idea I was going to be the principal participant in an unexpected and dramatic birth that Friday night as I followed my family into the huge auction hall and sat down in one of the long rows of chairs. Being fourteen years old, I naturally ignored my dad, mom, younger brother, and three younger sisters, who sat on my left, whispering and joking with a couple of boys from school on my right.

Having arrived in Canada as an immigrant just two years before, my dad eagerly had accepted the invitation from Eddie, a carpenter he worked with, to come to a weeklong series of free music concerts.

"It's a men's quartet, and some of the songs are in German," Eddie had said.*

My dad was not yet fluent in English, and since German was close to our native Dutch, he wanted to hear some German singing and maybe even talk with someone who spoke German—anything to get a break from two years of English immersion!

So nearly every night that week, our family came to the large hall and enjoyed the music. My family did not get much out of the preaching that followed, not being fluent in English, but that was a small price to pay for the great music. I understood and spoke English better than any of my family, but I had learned to tune out the preachers, especially the one we heard in our church on Sunday mornings. He never had anything to say that affected me.

Now it was Friday, the last night of the concert. The quartet stood up to sing, the pianist began a lively introduction, and they launched into their first song while I leaned back and relaxed to listen:

"As you travel along, on the Jericho road . . ."

I knew about Jericho and the mountainous road to Jerusalem, having heard Bible stories read at the dinner table every day since I was a little boy.

"Does the world seem all wrong, and heavy the load?"

Yes, I sometimes felt a load of fear. Just the week before, walking home from a neighbour, I had seen a blood-red setting sun. I had looked over my shoulder to see a luridly red full moon rising above the horizon. It looked as if it were dripping blood, just like the stories I had heard about the end of the world. I half expected to see the stars fall from the sky. I was afraid. Afraid to meet God. Afraid to die.

My mind focused again on the singing.

"On the Jericho road . . . "

"Yes," I thought, "the Jericho road is a picture of my life—plenty of troubles and challenges."

"On the Jericho road, there's room for just . . ."

"One," my mind filled in the next word. "There's room for just *one.*"

I knew life was not easy. I grew up during war time. Life was tough. I needed to be strong and use the power of a strong will to live life with its many challenges and problems.

And then the quartet sang the rest of the line:

"There's room for just *two.*"

"Two?" Who could that second person be? I had no idea, and I eagerly waited for them to sing the next line.

"On the Jericho road, there's room for just *two.* No more and no less, just *Jesus* and you."

Whoosh! Light! Understanding!

It was like the week before when I was playing hide and seek with my little brother and sister in a darkened barn and the farmer, without warning, flung open the huge doors. A blast of light and suddenly I could see everything clearly.

"Each burden He'll bear, each sorrow He'll share. There's never a care, 'cause Jesus is there."

"Yes! Yes! Yes! That's what I want! I need Jesus to walk life's road with me!"

In his sermon, the preacher explained how Jesus is the One who meets our every need. He forgives my sins. He gives me strength to live right, courage to meet life's problems, and at the end, He welcomes me to a home in Heaven. I heard truths I had never heard in church in Holland, nor in the church I attended in Canada. He concluded with, "If there is someone in this hall who needs Jesus to walk with Him on life's road, stand up and come down to the front. Someone will pray with you."

I stood immediately, pushed my way past my friends, and nearly ran to the front. There, on my knees, I confessed my sinfulness, my fears, and my need. I came to Jesus the best I knew how, and He accepted me. I was born into the kingdom of God. I stood up, a newborn baby, and returned to my friends and family. They did not know what to make of this strange behaviour, but they would learn, and eventually all my family came to know Jesus as their own personal Saviour.

Was it that simple little traditional spiritual song that brought me to Jesus? Of course not! It was merely the trigger. God's Holy Spirit had prepared me through years of hearing Bible stories. That song, no matter how well performed, would have meant nothing to me without that background.

I know that now, and I knew it then. That is why I was so open to get involved in bringing the Word of God to other people—first as a preaching pastor of a small church, next as a Bible translator in Brazil, then as a leader in Bible translation organizations, and now as a speaker and writer.

My passion is that everyone on earth, all 6.8 billion people, will have the chance to hear or read the life-giving stories of God's Word in the language they know best.

Canada's greatest gift to the world is still the story of Jesus—the One who is there as the second person on the road of life. It is Canada's gift to the world, as Canadian Christians pray and give and go to spread the Good News to the ends of the earth.

*The Janz Quartet was started by brothers of the Janz family of Herbert, SK, who attended Prairie Bible Institute and became an evangelistic team. Although they were Mennonites they said little about Mennonite, distinctive cultural and social practices, focusing on the need for conversion. By the early 1950s, they were in their heyday. From T.D. Regehr, *Mennonites in Canada: A People Transformed* (University of Toronto Press, 1996), 208-9.

A GARDEN IN YOUR POCKET

I have always been a book reader. Five years ago, I became a book writer, and now I have become a book seller. I speak at an average of sixty events each year and usually bring some books to sell. At the end of each banquet, meeting, or conference, I stand by my book table, greet the participants, and autograph the books they buy. Many people buy books, but many more do not, often giving me a variety of excuses.

"I just watch TV and DVDs," some say. "The best movie you will ever see," I tell them, "is the book you are reading because it's happening inside your own head." I am tempted to tell them that I often feel like Groucho Marx, who said, "I find television very educational. The minute somebody turns it on, I go to the library and read a good book."*

"I don't have time to read," is such a popular explanation that I sometimes jokingly say, "Buy my book, and for an extra $20, I'll pray that God will give you time to read." They laugh and respond, "No thanks, I might end up reading it in the hospital recovering from who knows what."

Hopefully this is all in good fun and not just a tactful way of them telling me, "I hated your speech, so no way will I buy your books!"

But one reason for not buying a book is anything but funny at all. "I'm not a reader," many people say, and not just my audiences either. Churches appear to be full of people who do not read much beyond a few verses of the Bible. They do not seem to realize that people who *do not* read are no better off than people who *cannot* read. Nor do they realize that being able to read good books is a gift from God. A billion people in the world have never had a chance to learn to read. God has given us who live in North America every opportunity to learn, and He will hold us accountable for what we have done with those opportunities. "From everyone who has been given much, much will be demanded" (Luke 12:48, NIV).

I used to tell my daughters (and now I tell everyone), "The two greatest influences in your life are the people you meet and the books you read. You *can't* control which people you meet, but you *can* choose what books you read." Rene Descartes, a sixteenth century philosopher, said something similar, "The reading of all good books is like a conversation with the finest men of past centuries."

Books are time travel machines—an unattainable technological fantasy. But we who are book readers know time travel is real. We can voyage back through the centuries and converse with people who have been dead a thousand years. We can journey faster than the speed of light to distant countries and live in long ago ages, learning firsthand the lifestyles and thoughts of ancient authors. As poet Emily Dickinson put it, "There is no frigate like a book / To take us lands away, / Nor any coursers like a page / Of prancing poetry."**

Books are bees, carrying ideas that cross-pollinate the minds of readers, fertilizing and bringing new ideas to life. As a result, readers of good books live life more fully, think more profoundly, and influence a wider range of people. We who are readers know that we can live more than one life. Through reading good books, we can live as many lives as we want.

I have been watching my grandchildren grow up. Their parents are constantly with them as they learn to walk, eat, and dress themselves. But when the kids discover books, they fly away, gone for hours in distant places and times, absorbed in other lives, far from their parents and home. Books give readers wings.

I am a pusher, I admit it. I push books. I pushed books for decades before I wrote my own. On every furlough speaking engagement I gave away or sold books.

One of my favourite authors, GK Chesterton, said, "There is a great deal of difference between an eager man who wants to read a book and a tired man who wants a book to read."*** Since my first three books are an eclectic collection of over one hundred and fifty columns, there is something for both the eager person wanting solid content and the tired one who wants to be entertained.

My wife is a gardener. She not only enjoys tending the numerous bushes and flower beds around our lakeside home, but she also brings in flowers to decorate the table or berries to serve with ice cream. She is physically and mentally healthier when she regularly spends time in her garden.

An Arab proverb says, "A book is a garden carried in the pocket."****

We who are book readers know what that means.

*"Groucho Marx Quotes." Brainy Quote. 2010: http://www.brainyquote.com/quotes/authors/g/groucho_marx_2.html

**"Emily Dickinson Quotes." Good Reads. 2010: http://www.goodreads.com/author/quotes/7440.Emily_Dickinson

***"G.K. Chesterton Quotes." Good Reads. 2010: http://www.goodreads.com/quotes/show/43362

****"Arabian Proverbs." World of Quotes. 2010: http://www.worldofquotes.com/proverb/Arabian/1

CLOTHING WARS

"She shouldn't be wearing that kind of outfit! Just look at that tight top! Those straps look like spaghetti! It just isn't Christian!"

I am getting tired of the way older church folk criticize young people for the way they dress. Give it a break, folks. Let's look at this issue biblically.

Back in the 19th century, Christians believed that for African men and women to be good Christians, they had to become "proper English gentlemen and ladies." This meant men had to dress in sturdy broadcloth suits and leather shoes, and the women had to wear dresses with bustles, or crinolines and petticoats. Christianity was equated with British culture—a most unbiblical concept!

A pastor once criticized me for wearing a "non-Christian" tie. He thought it was too bright, even though flashy ties were in fashion at that time. I was sorely tempted to enquire how we could bring my tie to repentance, but quietly changed ties since I was going to speak in his church.

At a mission conference workshop in another church, I asked the study group, "What is the purpose of clothing?"

Participants had dozens of answers: "To make ourselves look good. To fit in with the rest of our group. To show respect. To impress others. To protect our bodies from cold and harm, etc."

Then I asked, "What is the biblical purpose of clothing?" After much discussion, the consensus was that the biblical purpose was to show modesty.

My question, "So how should Christians dress?" provoked a storm of argument. That is when I told them the following story:

"Why aren't you out with your friends singing on the plaza this afternoon?" my wife asked our three little daughters who were hanging out in the shade of our mud-walled, palm-thatched house in the Canela village.

"We're not going anymore," Valorie announced. "Those old ladies are always slapping our feet," Leanne explained. "Yeah," preschool Cheryl added, "and it hurts!"

Now what? I thought. For months, our daughters had gone with other little girls to join the women's singing line on the plaza. They loved to imitate the young women as they sang shoulder to shoulder in the dance line, bending their knees and rocking their arms back and forth to the beat of the dance rattle as the young men danced in a group before them.

We investigated. "We're just teaching your girls to be modest," one of the older women said. What? Our girls were dressed exactly like the other girls and women—a wrapped skirt of coloured cloth covering them from waist to knees. How could this bare breasted Canela grandma accuse our little girls of being immodest?

More research, more explanations. Finally, we figured it out. All those bare breasted women and girls stood with their feet and knees touching. Our daughters stood with their ankles together, but with the front of their feet and their knees apart. This stance, combined with eye contact, said to the young men dancing in front of them, "Hey, I'm interested in you. Let's get together after the dance."

The grandmas sitting behind the line of girls were simply doing their job, making sure the girls kept their feet chastely together by a slap on the side of the offending foot.

I then asked the workshop group, "Can a Christian Canela girl be modest in the dancing line, even while bare breasted, as long as she keeps her feet and knees together?"

A long silence. Finally an elderly grandma on the front row spoke up. "Yes, she can!" she said firmly. "Modesty comes from the heart, and that is what God looks for. It doesn't matter how a girl shows her modesty as long as it is culturally appropriate."

Good for grandma!

How cultures indicate public modesty and reserve varies widely. Islamic groups prescribe coverings for women that may range from a simple headscarf *hijab* to a *burka* full body covering, leaving only a slit for the eyes. Some societies are particular about colour. Black and white, or dark blue are preferred, while bright colours are judged as too attention getting. Sometimes the "clothing" is nothing more than a gourd strapped over the man's penis, as is the custom among some highland communities in Papua New Guinea. Other societies caution men and women from making eye contact with each other to preserve modesty.

If God sees that we have geared our hearts and attitudes towards modesty, He does not care what kind of clothing we wear, or how we wear it, as long as it shows our modesty within our own culture. Decisions about clothing need to pass the biblical standard of modesty. After that, it is basic, common-sense wisdom that guides us.

I would be a fool to stand up in front of two-hundred well-dressed banquet guests while wearing scruffy, ill-fitting clothes and make a speech about the importance of Bible translation. My clothes would distract. No lawyer would go camping in his three-piece suit, nor would a wise person apply for a job as a bank teller dressed in ragged jeans and a grubby T-shirt.

Young people may need guidance to dress wisely for the occasion, but unless it is clearly an issue of modesty, we older folk have no right to bang them on the head with the Bible.

THROWN IN AT THE DEEP END

It happened the first time we went to a swimming pool in the summer of our first furlough in Canada. Cheryl, our youngest, was almost four years old when she ran out of the women's dressing room ahead of Jo and her sisters, and teetered on the edge of the deep end. The lifeguard instantly blew her whistle, shouted, "Grab that little kid!" and clambered hastily from her lookout perch. Too late. Grinning hugely, Cheryl jumped in and disappeared under the water.

I held up my hands to calm the lifeguard down, "Don't worry! She can swim! It's okay!

It really wasn't a problem. We had taught all three of our girls to swim in the deep and swiftly flowing river near the first Canela village we lived in when they were toddlers. Cheryl was ready for the deep end. But that is not the way life usually works. Often we find ourselves in the deep end of situations without a shred of preparation. How do we cope?

As a twenty-four-year-old new pastor, I was hunched over the tiny desk in the corner of our bedroom preparing my very first sermon, when there was a knock on the door. My visitors were a middle aged couple and their elderly mother who wanted me to come with them to see her eighty-five-year-old husband. Doctors had just diagnosed him with inoperable cancer, and he was not expected to live more than a few months. "He doesn't know he is dying," his wife told me, "and he is not a Christian." The couple added, "He also hasn't made his will yet."

I prayed a lot during that half-hour car ride. Stopping in front of a mobile home on the farmyard, the young woman opened the door, ushered me in and said, "Dad, this is the pastor. He needs to talk with you." Then they closed the door and left me in the deep end.

I sat down at the dinette table across from the old man and saw tears beginning to form in his eyes. I asked him, "Do you know what this is about?" He nodded, the tears now sliding down his cheeks. "How long do I have?" he asked. I told him. Then I opened my Bible and led him to faith in Jesus. After we prayed, I mentioned the will. "I will attend to it right away," he replied. Only two weeks later, we buried him. I had never even attended a funeral before, let alone had to tell someone he would die soon.

I survived those deep end experiences because I hung onto Jesus' promise, "I am with you always" (Matt. 28:20, NIV). I believed God was in control and that He would give me the wisdom and strength to keep my head above water and swim to shore.

God never puts us into a situation that we—together with Him—cannot handle. He always prepares us at least a little. For instance, when we started our ministry among the Canela and I moved my family into a palm leaf roofed house with a dried mud floor and walls, I felt we had jumped into the deep end. We had no electric power, gas, water, sewer, or phone. We could not communicate with the villagers, and there was nothing to read in the Canela language because there were no books—a great motivation to learn Canela as quickly as possible!

It was the deep end, but it was not a total shock. Eighteen years earlier, when I was twelve years old, my Dad moved his family from the Netherlands to Canada. We suddenly found ourselves living in abject poverty in cheap housing. We had no electric power, gas, water, sewer, or phone. We could not communicate with anyone, and I, who used to read three books a week in Holland, had nothing to read—a great motivation to learn English as quickly as possible!

Probably the deepest deep end experience was getting married. I felt utterly unprepared. Marriage for Jo and me was not a "let's try it and see how we like it" experiment. We conformed to the biblical standard of a once-and-for-all, life-long commitment. Social pressure also kept us together. Our families would not approve if we split, nor would any of our friends or colleagues. Besides, after we were in full-time ministry with Wycliffe, I realized a divorce would leave me financially destitute since Jo's friends were by far our best donors! (Juuust kidding!)

Although I felt utterly unprepared to be a husband, I had, of course, many thoughts and expectations about certain aspects of marriage that I was very happy to learn about first hand. For the most part, however, I had no idea how to act. I was called *Husband* many years before I actually learned how to behave in that role. Then the kids started coming, bringing more deep end experiences. Again, I was called *Daddy* long before I knew how to act as one. Through all these experiences, God kept my head above water.

Although I have been thrown into many deep ends, I have not yet had to face the kinds of situations some of my friends, partners, and colleagues are dealing with right now. For some, it is the death of a spouse or a child or sibling. For others, it is a deadly form of cancer in themselves or their spouse or child, a life-threatening illness, a heart attack or stroke, a disabling illness, an accident leaving them crippled for life, or the loss of a secure job, position, or income, etc.

Jesus Christ does not spare His followers deep end experiences, but He does keep His promise to be there with us and take us through.

"When you're in over your head, I'll be there with you. When you are in rough waters, you will not go down" (Isa. 43:2, *The Message*).

WHEN FACTS ARE NOT

On Tuesday, July 22, 1969, the day after Neil Armstrong became the first person to walk on the moon, the Canela elders' council summoned me to the plaza. They were worried. They had heard rumours about North Americans wanting to shoot a rocket up to the moon and land on it. I confirmed that the rocket had just landed and that, yes, people were walking on the moon.

"Write a letter to your chief and elders," the councillors ordered me. "Tell them not to walk on Putwry's belly. He won't like it and will cause all kinds of trouble. Maybe it'll rain at the wrong time, or not at all. Our gardens will fail, and we will all starve to death."

I tried to calm their fears by giving them an astronomy lesson, attempting to bring their ideas about the moon a little closer to the facts. It did not seem to help much. It sometimes takes a long time to move from believing a partial truth to accepting the full truth.

Twelve years later, I suffered a deep depression. That is when I should have remembered that the things one believes to be true may not be. There can be a huge difference, especially in theology, between perception and reality.

"God, I don't think you know what you are doing anymore!" I shouted, waving my arms at the sky. "Where's your wisdom? Where's your power? Where is your love? I half expected to be struck by lightning when I shouted those blasphemies into the sky, but God pitied me and brought a godly pastor into my life instead.

All during that dreadful period of deep depression and lack of faith, he let me tell him my story of deep frustration with God. He prayed for me and with me. He gave me Scriptures to read. He encouraged me to keep on with some of my spiritual disciplines. I did not preach, I did not write anything—I had nothing to say. As far as

I was concerned, God had let me down. But I kept reading the Bible regularly. I continued to pray, telling Him how I felt, frequently and at length. I kept giving to support other missionaries, and I kept listening to recorded hymns and going to church.

After six months of weekly counselling, I finally realized that I was not angry with God Himself: I was frustrated with the God of my perception. My view of the character of God and how He operates in the world was merely my inadequate understanding of Him, not the actual truth. I rejected the small God of my limited theology, not the infinite God Himself. I repented, and God forgave me, restoring my faith, my peace, and my joy.

Let's face it, God is huge, and He is complex! If all the theologians that ever lived could work together for a hundred years and put together a description of God, their depiction would still reflect only a tiny fraction of who God really is. The difference between the theologians' perception and reality would be astronomical.

The apostle Paul wrote, "We know only a portion of the truth, and what we say about God is always incomplete. . . . We don't yet see things clearly. We're squinting in a fog, peering through a mist. But it won't be long before the weather clears and the sun shines brightly. We'll see it all then, see it all as clear as God sees us, knowing him directly just as he knows us!" (1Cor. 13:9-12, *The Message*).

The fact that all Christians, even the wisest and most sincere, are merely "squinting in a fog and peering through a mist," has enormous implications for the outward unity of the Church in the world.

When it comes to a difference of opinion with another believer about God and His Kingdom, both parties need to be willing to say, "You may be right. I may be wrong. I don't think I am, but there is a possibility that I don't yet understand everything there is to know about this. My perception may not completely reflect reality."

That should not be too hard to do. We do it all the time in other areas. Every day we add to our knowledge about things around us. From mundane experiences like trying a new dessert, to the extraordinary one of getting married, we begin by forming perceptions. In the case of the dessert, our first few bites are often enough to turn our perceptions into full understanding of the reality;

the proof of the pudding is in the eating, but the proof of the marriage is in the living—for decades beyond the honeymoon!

The more complex the experience, the longer it takes to match our perceptions to reality. No wonder then, that experiencing God is a life-long project—and beyond. He is infinitely complex! When we are part of a community of faith, read His Word, pray, listen to Him, and serve Him by building his Kingdom of justice for all, we gradually learn more of who God really is.

When the Canelas finally learned the true nature of the moon, their fear of a moon walk causing starvation disappeared. When I finally realized God was far more complex than I had imagined, my doubt about God being in control vanished. Christians who recognize that God and His ways are far too complex to tuck neatly into a theological box promote unity in the Church as they hold their opinions lightly and in humility.

When God's people finally take in the extravagant dimensions of Christ's love for the world, not only will our fears and doubts evaporate, we will "live full lives, full in the fullness of God" (Eph. 3:19, *The Message*). That is when Jesus' prayer for His Church will be answered, "The goal is for all of them to become one heart and mind—just as you, Father, are in me and I in you, so they might be one heart and mind with us" (John 17:21, *The Message*).

HOT VALUE HIDDEN IN THE ASHES

They are called *Prohkam*—literally "In the ashes"—an apt name for Canela village elders since their hair is ash grey and their bodies take on a grey cast as the ashes from the evening campfires settle on them. Their main function is to pass along Canela cultural values to the next generation.

I learned a deeper meaning of this name when our three-year-old daughter stumbled home in tears. She and her friends and pre-school sisters had been playing in the remnants of an old campfire, using the charcoal to draw designs on each other's bodies, when she stepped on some glowing embers buried deeply in the cold ashes.

Glowing embers are dangerous. Not only do they char little feet, but they are also the fastest and most assured way of starting a new fire. During the winter months in Canada, all I have to do each morning is pile kindling onto the leftover glowing embers in our fireplace, and within minutes, a roaring fire radiates its welcome heat.

Cold ashes look used up and appear worthless. Many elderly people do too. But just as deep down inside the ashes the still glowing embers have the power to ignite new fires, so the deep down life wisdom of the elderly has the power to help young people live better, value driven lives.

The "In the ashes" Canela councillors do not lecture. Instead, they tell stories—oral tribal history, tales of their own youth, of their failures, and how they overcame them. Canela teens absorb concepts such as: work for what you need, work together with others, relationships are essential, respect the opinions of others, and be generous.

Unfortunately, North American young people usually do not get their values from their elders, but through their peers, movies, television shows, and song lyrics. There is little biblical life wisdom in these sources. Unlike the traditional Canela story telling on the village plaza, our society today does not have a good system of tapping into the wisdom of the elderly that is so desperately needed by our young people.

In our culture, it is difficult to bring the dry kindling into frequent contact with the glowing embers. We value extreme individualism: families often live separately and far from the grandparents. We tend to segregate the elderly from the younger. Strangely, we do this even in churches in spite of the biblical command in Titus 2 for older Christians to teach the younger ones how to live. How regularly do elderly men and women tell their life stories to children in Children's Church?

Wise elderly men and women in every culture not only have a lot to share, but they want to share it. Younger people need to recognize that they require the insights many older folk have. They need to ask questions of their elders about marriage and career, relationships, money management, and work skills. And the older folk need to respond—not with harangues, lectures, or criticism, but with personal stories full of biblical values and good examples to follow or, occasionally, bad ones to avoid.

When I was a novice Bible translator, I sat down with one of our Wycliffe veteran translators. He told me some of the things he had done, and I took notes. Then I asked him, "Knowing what you now know, if you were to do your translation program again, what would you do differently?" That's when his glowing embers of wisdom ignited my life's kindling!

Stories full of biblical values and good examples are, of course, not enough. Not one of us can live the way we ought to live without God's help. Here, too, the elderly have an important responsibility to pray for the young people that they have the opportunity to ignite. Both stories and prayer are needed for the embers to set the kindling ablaze.

→ COLUMN 33 ←
THE ARMY OF THE ELDERLY

In North America a hundred years ago, only one person in twenty-five was over sixty-five years old. Now, however, the ratio is 1:8, and in the next few decades, the number of older people will grow to a ratio of 1:5.*

Isn't it wonderful that this continent is being overwhelmed with elderly people, including, of course, elderly Christians? The more the better! Old Christians can be a rich spiritual resource.

Elderly believers can powerfully bless younger people in at least two ways: they can tell stories to pass on life values, inspire, and encourage younger people; and they can pray for them. After decades of knowing God, many elderly believers have a special intimacy with Him and are uniquely qualified to pray with power. They have vast life experience and can pray intelligently for all sorts of situations. They have seen startling answers to prayer and thus have the faith to pray for difficult problems.

A few generations ago, twenty-six-year-old John Wilbur Chapman became the pastor of the First Reformed Church in Albany, New York.** After the first Sunday, an elderly man came up to him and said, "Young man, you are much too young to be the pastor of such a prestigious church as this. But next Sunday I will come to church early with a friend and pray that God will fill you with His Holy Spirit and bless your ministry."

Every Sunday those two old men came to church early to pray. After a few weeks, there were five men, then ten, then fifty, and eventually two hundred men who showed up to pray for young pastor Chapman. In the next three years, over eleven hundred men and women came to faith in Christ because of that church's ministry. Pastor Chapman eventually became a highly effective evangelist, working with D.L. Moody and Billy Sunday.

Many years ago, I heard of four old guys who met every Monday in the local Tim Horton's coffee shop to rehash the Sunday church service over coffee and doughnuts. One day, one of them mentioned Jimmy, a talented seventeen-year-old member of the worship team. "I hear he is very conscientious about coming to practices," he said. The others agreed with him, mentioning other positive traits. Before they left, they thanked God for Jimmy and prayed for him.

Throughout the weeks following, they kept their ears open for information about Jimmy, and on Mondays prayed for this teenager, eventually asking God to use him in full time ministry.

After six months, one of the elderly men accosted Jimmy after church and asked him if he wanted to come to lunch with them. "Any restaurant you want, anything on the menu," he offered. It sounded good to Jimmy, so he accepted the invitation, though he wondered what four old codgers could want with him.

During the meal, they astounded Jimmy with their questions and comments, showing they knew all about his favourite subjects at school, his girlfriend, his part-time job, and his passion for volleyball. But he was even more surprised when they told him that they had been praying for him for six months, and that they felt that God wanted him in full time ministry. Jimmy didn't know what to think. "We will commit to pray for you faithfully for the rest of our lives," they said.

Ten years later, when the last of the old men died, Jimmy was a senior in seminary. He is now in full time ministry.

When I told this story at a home prayer meeting, a teenage girl suddenly began to cry. "I wish somebody would do that for me," she sniffed through her tears. That same week, while speaking at a chapel service in a seminary, I asked, "How many of you students have had elderly people, not your relatives, come up to you and say, 'I will pray for you faithfully while you are in seminary?'" Out of several hundred students, only five put up their hand. "The elderly in your churches have failed you," I told the rest of the students.

Korean churches, however, do not fail their seminary students—they take prayer seriously. For decades we have heard reports of 75 percent of church members, including thousands of elderly people, coming together daily to pray in early morning meetings all over the country. Surely seminary students are on their prayer list!

What are the results? Very few Korean churches divide because of conflict or disagreements: they split because they have grown too large for the location. Korean pastors falling into immorality is a phenomenon practically unheard of. A huge seminary in Seoul with over twelve hundred students turns away hundreds of applicants each year. No wonder the Korean Church is sending out a growing number of missionaries to serve cross-culturally all over the world!

Bible readers are familiar with many hundreds of passages exhorting God's people to pray for themselves and for others. The world does not need more knowledge about prayer; it desperately needs more practice of prayer. And that is exactly where elderly people fit in.

Churches need to honour their elderly as rich spiritual resources and mobilize these storytellers and prayer warriors. The number of the elderly is growing, and I can hardly wait to see what miracles God is going to perform in North America as they inspire younger people with their stories and empower them with their prayers.

*Mark H. Beers, ed. *Merk Manual of Geriatrics*. 2000. Revised 2006. Whitehouse Station, N.J: Merck & Co., Inc.

http://www.merck.com/mkgr/mmg/sec1/ch2/ch2b.jsp

**"John Wilbur Chapman, 1859-1918, Evangelist." Believer's Web. 2003. http://www.believersweb.org/view.cfm?ID=116

⊹ COLUMN 34 ⊱
MOVE IT, MOVE IT, MOVE IT

You know what bugs me the most in my work as a recruiter for missionaries? It's when people misapply the Bible's warnings not to trust ourselves. I get so tired of young people asking, "I know what I would like to do with my life, but how can I know it is God's will?"

Then they quote Proverbs 3:5: "Trust in the Lord with all your heart, and lean not on your own understanding" (NIV). Sometimes they add, "I think what I want to do is the right thing, but I'm not sure. Maybe I am just being '. . . wise in my own eyes'" (Prov. 3:7).

Okay, I know what they are getting at. Proverbs is loaded with advice to trust God and not ourselves. Jesus often told stories about the danger of people trusting in themselves, their spiritual position, or their plans and ideas without a thought of God. We all remember the one about the farmer who, after harvesting a bumper crop, planned to take it easy for the rest of his life—which ended that night (Luke 12:17–19).

But when Christians apply these principles wrongly, they immobilize themselves. God does not tell us to sit and twiddle our thumbs while waiting for Him to tell us specifically what good thing to do next. At the least He wants us to pray for wisdom to discover our strengths and to make major life decisions: "If any of you lacks wisdom, you should ask God, who gives generously to all without finding fault, and it will be given to you" (James 1:5, NIV).

But many of the people I talk with have already done that. They recognize what they are good at and what they like to do. They are ready to make sacrifices in order to go to the mission field and help meet deep needs. But they still ask, "How can I know that it is God's will, and not just my own desire?"

A godly young couple asked me that question one day. They had strong, well-developed talents and giftings, and were highly competent in a number of skills desperately needed on the foreign mission field. They were willing to raise their own financial support and leave home and friends to go. They said, "We want to do cross-cultural missions work, but how can we be sure it is God's will?"

I answered, "Look, there's your little daughter, riding her tricycle. Let's say that in another month she gets too big for it. So you buy her a little two-wheeler, put on the training wheels, teach her to put on her helmet, and help her to ride up and down the driveway. After a while, do you think your daughter will say to herself, 'I just love riding my new two-wheeler, but I wonder if daddy really wants me to?'"

What utter nonsense! Of course she knows you want her to! Why else would you have given her a bike and helmet? Why else would you be encouraging her as she rides down the driveway? Well then, do you think God would treat you any differently? So why do you keep wondering if God wants you in a place where you can use the experience, talents, and skills He has given you to build His Kingdom?"

I want to tell folk like that to stop quoting Proverbs and get with it. I want them to "Move it! Move it! Move it!" the way Trinidad and Tobago rapper The Mad Stuntman sang in the Madagascar movies our grandkids love to watch.*

Now, before you decide I am a heretic and start looking for incendiary materials, let me clarify something. I certainly am not saying we should forget about listening to further direction from God. He is sovereign. He knows the future. We don't. He is in charge. We aren't. A few years ago, I was driving peacefully along a busy street in Edmonton when someone in a heavy Mercedes sports utility vehicle roared through a stop sign and T-boned me on the passenger side. End of the car; end of the trip. Fortunately Jo was not with me or it would have been the end of her. Let's face it, we can't even be sure we will make it back from the grocery store safely.

Life is uncertain. But God is still in charge. With Him there is no uncertainty. So we can confidently move ahead in our lives. I advise people who are making the decision to move into a missions career or who are thinking of going on a major missions trip to pray something like this:

"God, you are in charge. You gave me the abilities that I can use to advance Your work on earth. You even gave me the desire to get going. So I am going to move ahead, and if You want me to stop, You can do so. Or You can guide me into a different direction. It's up to you. But I'm going to get moving."

Jo and I were moving towards a ministry in mass evangelism in Europe when God diverted us into twenty-four years of Bible translation in Brazil. Pretty radical change, but no problem. We just kept moving. After that, He moved us into a public speaking ministry, and from there to nine years of leadership, and now into more speaking and writing. Fine with us. We just want Him to use us to the max.

And for those of you who are still sitting there pondering, I have a few words: Move it! Move it! Move it!

*Mark Quashie and Eric Morillo, *I Like to Move It* (Strictly Rhythm, 1994).

❖ COLUMN 35 ❖
SIX-POINT-SIX BILLION BELIEVERS

Some atheists are even better than stand-up comedians at making me laugh. They ridicule the idea of faith in God, denying He exists, yet they are so humorously full of faith in the way they live the rest of their lives.

A couple of books published recently, *The God Delusion* and *God is Not Great*, once again state that smart people do not believe in anything that cannot be checked, verified, and proven in a physical, material, time and space way. That, of course, includes God. Christians say, "God is." Atheists say, "Prove to me that God exists, and prove it to me using scientifically verifiable methods that I will accept. Without these, I can't believe."

Faith-rejecting atheists are like fish that reject the concept of water. Faith surrounds them every moment of their lives. God designed all human beings, including atheists, to live our practical, everyday lives by having faith in things we cannot prove. Since we cannot possibly know everything, we have to believe what others tell us is true. Since we must continue to live our daily lives without being able to prove everything in a physical, material, time and space way, we are forced to act by faith.

I think of that whenever I drive our little motor home south through the mountains to San Jose, California, to spend some time with our oldest daughter and her family (and to get away from the snow, the phone, and the house maintenance so I can write and study). Every hour, we meet hundreds of north bound vehicles passing within a few metres of us at a combined speed of 200 kilometres per hour (160 mph).

I ask myself, "How do I know the vehicle roaring towards me will stay in its own lane? How many of these drivers are arguing with someone on their cell phones? Which one of these drivers is drunk, or is falling asleep, or has just lost his job, or is returning from his child's funeral, or has just broken up with her boyfriend, or was told he has cancer, or just became engaged?"

As an expert driver, I am fully alert, although I may be talking with Jo or pondering whatever I am currently writing, but how do I know that other drivers will not suddenly swerve in my direction? Even though I cannot prove that the next two tons of steel hurtling north will not veer and smash into me, I keep driving. Why? By faith. Although I do not know the statistics, I believe that the risk is worth the goal. So do atheists. Yes, they too drive cars by faith, even on narrow snow-covered mountain roads, with no proof that the next semi-trailer truck they meet will stay on its side of the road.

By faith, people ride elevators and fly in airplanes, not knowing the slightest thing about the condition of the elevator cables, the plane's engines, or the pilot. By faith, people lie on operating tables to be cut open by fallible human doctors. By faith, people say "I do" and commit themselves to live for life with a person they are only beginning to know.

By faith, atheists, and all other people all over the world—6.8 billion of us—conduct businesses, operate machinery, take medications, invest money, ride ferries, and travel in buses. Most of these situations are without a shred of proof that the cheque is good, that the machinery won't blow up, that the medicine will work, that the bank won't fail, that the ferry won't sink, or the bus won't crash.

If every one of us insisted on scientifically verifiable proof on everything we now take by faith, no one would get out of bed in the morning, and we would all starve to death waiting for proof that our breakfast is safe to eat.

Some scientists, in spite of being astrophysicists and cosmologists, are atheists. I wonder how they feel when they are forced to accept the existence of matter they cannot see, measure, or describe. They do not know what this invisible stuff is. They can only infer its existence by what it does. They call it "dark matter."* No telescope can see it, nor does it emit or reflect enough electromagnetic radiation to be observed or measured. Dark matter can only be inferred from its gravitational effect on galaxies. No scientist knows what it consists of, yet believes that it makes up most of the universe. No proof, just faith through inference.

Christians could argue for the existence of God by the same inference. Jesus compared the Spirit of God to the wind. "The wind blows wherever it pleases. You hear its sound, but you cannot tell where it comes from or where it is going. So it is with everyone born of the Spirit" (John 3:8, NIV). We can see what God has made, how He responds to prayer, how He acts in the world today, and we could infer from this that God exists.

From there it is only a small step to saying, "God is." And from there it is only another small step to saying, "Since God is, and since He made us capable of being aware of Him, would He not want to communicate with His creatures?"

God does want us to know Him. ". . . anyone who comes to him [God] must believe that he exists and that he rewards those who earnestly seek him" (Heb. 11:6, NIV). That is the reason the Bible exists. It is a set of written stories and statements in which God progressively reveals His character and actions to the people He created—a most excellent reason to make sure that this Book is translated into the language of every human being on earth!

When I hear of atheists demanding proof that God exists, I wonder how they would answer if they were asked, "Would you prove to me that God cannot exist?" They would be stuck. They refuse to accept anything that might infer His existence and simply believe He does not exist. They have to take it by faith. Funny, it takes a lot of faith to be an atheist.

*NASA's *Imagine the Universe* Dark Matter: An Introduction

http://imagine.gsfc.nasa.gov/docs/science/know_l1/dark_matter.html

HUNGRY FOR GOD

The German university professor shook his head in bewilderment. "Jack," he blurted out, "You are well-educated, yet you believe in God! I have never met anyone like you."

The scene was a village of Canela people in the interior of Brazil in the mid-eighties. The professor was middle-aged, multi-lingual, with several academic degrees and plenty of international lecturing experience. He had come to visit and study in the Canela's village and was delighted with my willingness to share freely my expertise in the culture and language. Eventually the conversation got around to our spiritual motivation and Bible translation. That is when the thoroughly secularized professor was shocked to realize Jo and I were Christians with university educations. To him "educated Christian" is an oxymoronic statement on the level with "flat-earth astronomer." They just do not go together.

That German academic typifies the opinion of many other people in Europe. And no wonder! For decades, Europe has been on a drive to secularize society and marginalize God and the Bible. Holland, the country of my birth, is the continent's most notoriously liberal country. That is why countless Dutch immigrants all across Canada have told me, "It was economically hard for us in Holland right after the War," but they go on to say that now they are glad since the hardship drove them to emigrate to Canada, where they found a new life—not just economically, but spiritually.

Nearly one million Canadians claim full or partial Dutch ancestry. Most of them, like my family, arrived as post-war immigrants in the late forties and early fifties. Tens of thousands became born-again Christians in Canada.

Why could people not find God in the Netherlands in those years? After all, the land is filled with churches and cathedrals, their spires evident on every horizon. The focus of these liberal churches, however, was not on evangelism, but on social action. There were Christian labour unions and political parties, Christian schools, and radio stations, but they never said a word about a boy's need for a personal relationship with Jesus. Liberal theology was no match for the drive to secularize Europe.

But starting about ten years ago, things in the Netherlands began to change. According to Joshua Livestro, columnist for the Netherlands' largest selling newspaper, *De Telegraaf,* Dutch young people are turning to God and the Bible, and are they forming local Christian groups in surprising numbers.*

Recently, Livestro wrote in a major feature article that liberal churches, both Protestant and Roman Catholic, have been emptying out for decades, but that Christianity is alive and well outside the walls of these churches. In the past ten years, one hundred and twenty thousand people learned about the basic tenets of Christianity through the Dutch version of the *Alpha Course,* which introduces participants to Christianity. About one hundred new groups per year are springing up in related courses such as *Prison Alpha, Business Alpha, Student Alpha, Youth Alpha,* and the *Alpha Marriage Course.*

Informal youth churches are starting all over the country. At one time, there were forty-five of these new churches filled with about ten thousand young people. Two years later, twenty thousand young people pack into eighty-eight churches each week. In the city of Amersfoort, a group leader hired a hall that would hold five hundred people. To his surprise, eight hundred and fifty people packed into the first meeting. Now, twelve hundred young people show up regularly for two services per night.

Non-denominational house churches now operate in at least two hundred Dutch cities. One initiator organized a series of twelve regional seminars for people interested in house churches. He expected a small group of ten or twelve people per meeting; instead, more than fifty people showed up at each of the seminars.

It is not just among charismatic protestant groups where hunger for God is growing. The head master of a Roman Catholic secondary school in Rotterdam observed, "For years pupils were embarrassed about attending Mass. Now, they volunteer to read poems or prayers, and the school auditorium is packed."

In 2005, Holland's most prestigious literary prizes were awarded to openly Christian authors for books dealing in a sympathetic way with Christian issues of faith and redemption. One sold nearly three hundred and fifty thousand copies in the first year, making it the single bestselling Dutch-language book of the past decade.

No, that's not quite true.

One other book continues to outsell every other book. It is the *De Nieuwe Bijbelvertaling* (NBV), a new Dutch Bible translation which has sold a million copies since it was published in 2004. That is one NBV Bible for every sixteen people.**

This is no coincidence.

It is the Holy Spirit who makes people hungry for God, and He generates that God-hunger as people read His Word, the Bible, in their own heart language.

The written Word of God is the flashlight in the hand of the Holy Spirit to light our path to the Living Word of God, Jesus Christ.

That is why I am so passionate and excited about Bible translation.

Bible translation is the most foundational missions work still left for the worldwide Church to do. It took a well-educated Christian couple to do it for the pre-Christian Canela people of Brazil. It took a committee of God-fearing scholars to do it for the post-Christian Dutch people of Holland.

It will take thousands of committees of nationals, trained in translation, and helped by well-educated consultants, to do it for two hundred million people, speaking two thousand languages all over the world. My prayer and passion is to help complete this worldwide task.

The waves of Bible-driven hunger for God are already starting to spread from Holland into Germany. I wonder what my friend, the university professor, will think when students graduate not only well-educated, but fervently believing in God.

---

*Joshua Livestro. "Holland's Post-Secular Future: Christianity is dead. Long live Christianity!" WeeklyStandard.com. Vol. 12, 2007:

http://www.weeklystandard.com/Content/PublicArticles/000/000/013/110vxfxj.asp

**"New Bible translation Sells One Million Copies." Expatica.com. 2010: http://www.expatica.com/nl/news/dutch-news/New-Bible-translation-sells-one-million-copies_57333.html

"Europe's Christian Comeback." Foreign Policy. 2010: http:// www.foreignpolicy.com/story/cms.php?story_id=3881

✦ Column 37 ✦
It Hurt. But It Was Worth It

Coming home from the hospital with a new hip is not the same as coming home with a new baby. But according to my wife, there are similarities—like being willing to suffer pain in order to receive a greater joy.

It reminded me of an incident in my speaking ministry. A few years ago, I spoke at a number of Chinese churches in greater Vancouver. I encouraged the bright, articulate English-speaking Chinese young people to get involved in cross-cultural missions. And, using Cantonese and Mandarin interpreters, I also challenged the older Chinese Christians to make the sacrifice of giving their children to God to become missionaries—not easy for any parent.

One Sunday morning, as I was shaking hands at the door, a young mother came with her little son, Elisha.* "Pastor Jack," she said, "we would like a picture of you on the steps in front of the pulpit."

A few minutes later, I sat down in front of the pulpit with the young mother and her little son, while her husband started his video camera as he sat in a pew facing us.

The mom looked directly into the camera and said, "Elisha, you are now still too young to understand, but we will someday show you this video when you are older. Today is a special day. Today your daddy and I dedicated you to God to become a missionary. This man sitting next to you was the one whom God used to speak to us during these last few days."

By this time, tears were already beginning to sting my eyes. It is not easy for any parent to let their child go live and work in some far-off country. But it is particularly difficult for Chinese parents to give up their dreams for their children—not just that they will be well-educated, with healthy bodies, and have a secure career, but that their children and grandchildren will live nearby and be financially prosperous. These goals are highly valued in Chinese culture, but they are not always feasible if the children get involved in cross-cultural missions.

About a year later, I told this story to a Chinese church in Calgary as I spoke at their missions conference. After I sat down, the pastor invited young people who were willing to become cross-cultural missionaries to come to the front of the church and have their picture taken with me. Fifteen young people joined me in front of the pulpit.

"I will give each of you a copy of the picture to remind you of the commitment you have made today," the pastor said.

I sent an email to Elisha's mom to let her know how her action had moved others, and I received this reply:

> Pastor Jack, thank you for telling me this story. We are so encouraged. A few weeks ago, almost exactly a year after the Sunday we dedicated our son to God to be a missionary, Elisha woke me up around three o'clock in the morning. He then told me what had happened to him that afternoon in kindergarten.
>
> He was in the playground with all the other little kids, when suddenly the sky above him opened up, and a yellow light shone down. Then a big voice said, "I am God, and Elisha is my servant." Then the yellow light disappeared and everything was normal again. "And, mommy," he said, "God spoke in Cantonese!"
>
> After he told me his story, he went back to bed, but the next morning at breakfast, he told his daddy the same story, complete with full details. That evening at the bedtime Bible reading, I asked him, "Are you willing to be God's servant?" He said, "Yes!" and we prayed together that God would make him His child and his servant.

Jo and I did not understand what a sacrifice it was for our parents to let us go to Brazil as missionaries. They sacrificed much more than we did. We were young, idealistic, and excited about moving to a new country, learning new languages, and starting a new career. We didn't feel the pain of separation our parents felt. My parents lost their oldest son, their only daughter-in-law, and their only grandchildren—the youngest of which was only four months old. Jo's folks lost their only daughter and her family.

But twenty-four years later, my parents and Jo's mom joined us in the Canela village to participate in a festival for the distribution of a partial translation of the Bible in the Canela language. After the ceremonies were over, our parents reminisced.

"We stood in that Edmonton airport," my dad said, "and watched your plane until it disappeared. We cried, knowing we would not see any of you again for four years."

"Oh, it hurt to have you gone for so long," Jo's mom said.

"It hurt," they kept saying, "but it was worth it. Today, to see the Canelas receive God's Word in their own language. Oh, yes, it was worth all the pain."

"Jesus . . . who for the joy set before him endured the cross" (Heb. 12:2, NIV).

May God give little Elisha's parents, and others like them, a clear vision of the joy they will experience someday. It will help them endure the pain of separation from their missionary children, the pangs of loneliness, and the distress they feel when their children and grandchildren go through difficult times.

"It hurt," they will say, "but it was worth it."

*name changed to preserve privacy

✦ Column 38 ✦
It's All about Market Share

My wife and I once made a major investment—so did our families and friends. We invested twenty-five years of our lives in providing the Canela people of Brazil with a partial Bible in their own language. While we lived and worked in the Canela village for most of those years, our daughters lived in boarding school in Belem, one thousand kilometres away over bad roads. Our financial supporters gave nearly a million dollars while other partners prayed for decades to help us complete the project.

"Why?" we are often asked. "Why this huge investment just to put the Bible into Canela when there are only a few thousand speakers?"

A German university professor visiting the village once asked us that same question. As I shared our research with him, we conversed in English or Portuguese. He wondered why we taught the Canelas to read and write in their own language. "Why not just help them improve their ability in Portuguese," he would say. In vain, I tried to explain the value of the mother language, but the day he left, he unwittingly proved my point.

Having said goodbye to the villagers he turned to us and put his hands on my shoulders. Looking deep into my eyes, he said in English, "Jack, I want to say something to you, but I need to say it in my own language."

Switching to German, he said, "Thank you for investing so much of your life to serve the needs of the Canelas." Since German is closely related to Dutch, my own language, I could understand him well enough. "You have saved countless lives through your medical work. You have taught them how to read and to do arithmetic. Your work here prepared the Canelas to meet the inevitable coming of civilization on their own terms." By this time his eyes welled with tears, and he hugged me farewell.

As he drove off, I thought, "You've just proved my point. When you needed to express your deep feelings, you had to switch to your own language. God too has a deeply emotional message of love for the Canelas. You've just encouraged me to do whatever it takes to translate it into the Canela's own language."

If we evangelize a group of people who only partially understand the Good News, then we get a group of baby Christians who cannot grow up. How can they become disciples of their Rabbi, Jesus, without studying His life in their own language? How can missionaries plant self-sustaining churches without the Scriptures in the language of the people?

Bible translation is, therefore, the foundation of all missionary work. Jesus spoke Aramaic, the language spoken in Palestine at that time. The first translators, therefore, were Matthew, Mark, Luke, and John, who took the stories Jesus told in Aramaic and translated them into Greek—the most common language in the Mediterranean area. Christianity spread all through the Greek-speaking world because the Bible was available in Greek. Christian churches tend to grow strong and spread when the Scriptures are translated in the heart language of the people.

So what is the current status of worldwide Bible translation? There is both good news and bad news. Here are some round number statistics:

Almost 7,000 languages are spoken around the world today. Nearly 2,500 languages have either a full Bible or a New Testament translation. About 2,000 languages are currently having the Scriptures translated into them.*

The good news is that the 4,500 languages who either have, or soon will have, some of the Bible translated into them, comprise 97 percent of the world's population. They may not have a Bible in hand, or be able to read it if they had, but at least it is available in their language.

Most business people would be delighted if they had 97 percent of market share.

God is not! He wants 100 percent of market share! Jesus emphasized this in His parable of the shepherd with the hundred-sheep flock of which one was lost. That shepherd was concerned for the one lost sheep and focused his whole attention on going after that last 1 percent.

The Bible stresses 100 percent of market share. There are over 160 references throughout the Bible to nations, tribes, languages, and peoples with the adjective *all* or *every* in front of them.

The Psalms are filled with references to God being praised by *every* people group even from the ends of the earth. The Christmas angels proclaimed great joy for *all* people (Luke 2:10). The multitudes worshiping God will come from *every* tribe and language, *every* people group and nation (Rev. 5:9, 7:9). Jesus specifically instructed His disciples to make disciples of *all* nations (Matt. 28:19, Acts 1:8).

Now for the bad news: The 3 percent of the world's population still without any part of the Bible speak well over 2,000 different languages. What's more, many of these groups live in countries dominated by other world religions. Just like that one lost, hard-to-rescue sheep, so these language groups are in hard-to-access places.

Jesus, the Great Shepherd, has commissioned us, His followers, to reach even these hard-to-reach minority groups with God's salvation message in their own language.

It will not be easy. It will cost staggering amounts of money, many years of prayer, and the investment of hundreds of decades of lives. But it *must* be done. God *must* have 100 percent of market share.

How else will some from *every* people group on earth worship Him?

---

*"Facts and Figures." Wycliffe Bible Translators of Canada. 2010. http://www.wycliffe.ca/translation/language_stats.html

→ COLUMN 39 ←
JUST TAKE THE PLUNGE!

"Daddy, so when *are* we going back to Brazil?" our ten-year-old daughter Cheryl asked—not for the first time. I did not blame her. It was a cold Canadian January. She wanted to be back where it was warm, and she missed her friends on the mission centre.

I tried to explain, "I am taking some courses at the university college, and we still have more people to visit. Furlough is usually ten months, but it looks like we may have to stay longer. We just can't seem to save enough money to buy plane tickets."

That moved thirteen-year-old Valorie to ask, "How much more money do we need?" That is when we made a thermometer chart, graduated in hundreds of dollars, and taped it to the dining room wall. At the top Leanne, our middle daughter, printed, "Brazil Here We Come!"

The small red part at the bottom showed how little travel money we had been able to save during our first five months of furlough. Every day as we sat down to eat, the thermometer silently told us to remind God that we still needed more money. Every month we extended the red just a tiny bit higher.

In March, I got a phone call from an old friend in another province inviting me to be the keynote speaker at their weeklong missions conference two weeks before Easter.

"Archie," I replied, "There is no way I can do that. I have several papers to write for my courses. I have to study for two pre-Easter exams, and I have a ton of personal letters to write to our financial supporters to go out with our Easter newsletter. I can't spend a week with you, especially at that time. Besides, it takes all day to drive there from here. No way, I can't do it."

Archie, however, was prepared. "You won't need to drive. I'll send you plane tickets. You'll be staying in our house, so you will have a quiet place to study and write letters."

"God is my booking agent," I had often said. Now was the time to act on it. I breathed a quick prayer, "God, here we go then," took the plunge, and said, "Okay, I'll do it."

Monday afternoon, some weeks later, I found myself alone in Archie's home with my briefcase full of work. Archie was at his real estate office, and his wife was at school teaching. I was left alone to prepare for the first meeting. That evening, my talk went well, and I visited with people until nearly midnight.

The next morning I got up, found coffee ready and a note from my hosts: "See you tonight." I spent the entire day working, completely uninterrupted. No phone, no visitors. Nothing but work and study. That night I had another meeting and more visits until midnight.

The next day was the same routine. By Friday the course papers were completed, and I was fully prepared for my pre-Easter exams. The newsletter was written, and my correspondence was done. I was all set for the last presentation that night.

After the meeting, the treasurer handed me a large brown grocery bag and said, "Here is the offering. I've already taken out the hall rental fees. All the rest is yours." Without looking into the bag, I rolled it up to make a parcel, and when I got back to the house, I stuck it in my briefcase.

The next day I arrived home just as the girls were coming in from school. "Hey, Daddy's home! Did you bring us something, Daddy?"

"Yeah, I brought you something alright. Gather around."

With the whole family standing in the living room, I took the brown paper bag out of the briefcase, opened it, and held it high above my head. "This is what God gave me to bring to you!" I said and turned it upside down.

Flutter-flutter, tinkle-tinkle! Money all over the floor! Coins bouncing and rolling everywhere! Bills and cheques scattering like fallen leaves.

"Wow, look at all that money!"

"I'll count the tens and twenties."

"OK, I'll do the cheques."

"Cheryl, you collect the coins."

We counted the offering right there on the floor, and while still on our knees, we thanked God for His provision.

After the *Amen*, we trooped into the dining room. I grabbed the big red felt-tip pen and filled in the rest of the thermometer all the way to the top, with some red even spurting out the top!

The next morning, Jo booked the "Brazil Here We Come!" flights for the first week after school ended.

In the thirty years since then, every time I am asked to do something way beyond what I think I can do, I remember Archie, the thermometer chart, and the brown paper bag.

COLUMN 40
THE DAY GRANDMA BLEW IT

To autograph copies of my first two books *A Poke in the Ribs* and *A Kick in the Pants* is both a delight and a strain. It's a delight since it means someone liked the book well enough to pay money for it, and autographing it almost makes me feel like a real author. It is a strain because it involves writing legibly, something I have never been able to do to anyone's satisfaction.

It reminds me of an experience I had as a boy which made an indelible impression on my mind, and from which I learned a pivotal lesson—a lesson that helped me make major life decisions, such as getting involved in missions and Bible translation.

I was twelve years old when my family immigrated to Canada. I was thrilled with the numerous and vast changes from the crowded city life in tiny, cramped Holland. We lived in an old Alberta farmhouse surrounded by miles and miles of green and yellow grain fields, interspersed with spruce and poplar groves filled with what seemed to me strange animals and birds. I delighted in a two-month long summer vacation with perfect weather. What a welcome contrast to the mere first-two-week-in-August summer vacation I was used to in the Netherlands!

Each week my Mom and Dad wrote a letter to relatives in Holland, and each week they received one and read it aloud to each other. One day my Mom suggested I write a letter to my *Oma*, my grandmother. I eagerly accepted the suggestion. For months, I had already been writing letters in my head to relatives and friends back in the Netherlands.

I filled many pages, telling *Oma* about the two-mile cross-country walk with my little sister to the one-room schoolhouse and how I liked learning new English words there every day and teaching them to my Mom and Dad. I told about how I pumped and hauled pails of water to the house, gathered and chopped wood for the cook stove, and cleaned out the ashes in the morning. I described the scary howling of coyotes at night and the fun of hunting gophers in the fields with my slingshot. I wondered how she would respond to the feelings and experiences of her oldest grandson.

Some weeks later, a letter from *Oma* arrived. I listened closely as Dad read it to Mom while she was making supper. Then came the closing, *Veel liefs van Moeder*, "Much love from Mother," and a P.S. scribbled along the side, "I see Jack's penmanship is as bad as ever."

That evening I swung my axe slowly, methodically, and viciously splitting a spruce log into kindling.

A few weeks later, my Mom again invited me to write *Oma*. "I have scratched her off my list," I replied. I never wrote to *Oma* again, nor to any of my Dutch aunts and uncles. Obviously an auto-protective overreaction. But *Oma's* little one-line postscript also taught me a valuable lesson:

> I need input and advice from other people. But if those to whom I look for encouragement or advice get things wrong by focusing on the wrong aspect of a situation, I need to ignore their criticism.

My *Oma* should have concentrated on the content, not the form, of that first letter from her oldest grandchild. I poured out my heart on those pages, but all she saw was ink.

During the years that followed, people sometimes gave me advice stemming from a wrong focus. A church-going uncle, a fellow immigrant whom I respected, told me, "You'll soon get over this 'being saved' at that evangelistic crusade. After a few months, you'll just go to church on Sundays and live like the rest of us during the week."

A choirmaster told me, "You can't sing," and refused to let me join the high school choir. Others counselled me against attending Bible school, marrying Jo (can you believe it!), taking a pastoral position, going to Brazil as missionaries, living with the Canelas, considering a leadership position in Wycliffe, and writing weekly email columns.

This advice came from well meaning friends—focused on things like my family's health, our physical and emotional comfort, and our financial and material security. Those aspects, however, were irrelevant to us since we were ready to risk our health, comfort, and security in order to do something significant for God and mankind. When we received these bits of advice, we ignored them because we suspected they came from a wrong focus.

Jo and I tested each recommendation against what God was telling us through His written Word. We compared it with what the Holy Spirit was saying to us in our hearts, and we went to advisors whom we had learned to trust for the counsel we needed.

We all need trusted advisors, people who know us well and focus on the real issue—people who see the heart's blood, not the ink.

A lesson for us all: Neither offer, nor accept, advice based on the wrong focus.

WHAT'S SO HOLY
ABOUT THE BIBLE?

After ten years of study and work among the Canelas, we had a major problem. Each time we translated a Bible story about some miracle of Jesus and read it to Canelas, they would nod their heads and someone would say, "Great story, now let me tell you one of our stories." Then the Canela would tell an old-time myth of magic and talking animals. We would nod and say, "Great story. But the one we told you is different. Jesus really lived. This really happened."

We just could not get them to understand that the Bible stories we were translating were special. Everyone in our North American society knows that the term *holy* describes something having to do with God, or at least something with special religious significance. The Canela language and culture, however, have no such concept. To the villagers, the Bible stories were in the same class as the stories their grandfathers told them.

We prayed that God would do something to solve this problem, and He did, but in a painfully convoluted way.

We were planning to publish a number of booklets and books when a political upheaval in Brazil interrupted our work. Government policies changed and all missionaries working with indigenous people groups were forced to leave the villages and reservations. We too had to leave our home and friends in the village and live in the city for several years. It was emotionally painful and extremely frustrating for both us and for the Canela people, many of whom were eager to learn to read better. After several years, we published about a dozen booklets in Canela including some learn-to-read booklets, some booklets of traditional Canela legends, some health booklets, and the first versions of the translated books of Luke and Acts. We applied for permission to make a brief trip to the Canela village to deliver the reading books, sending the government department a list and description of the titles we planned to leave there.

Many weeks later, I was summoned to the district government office. The official handed me the document allowing me one day to distribute the books in the Canela village. Then he pointed to the bottom sentence; I looked and blinked in surprise. We had planned to give all this literature to the readers in the village—at least one per house—and had anticipated no major trouble. But there it was, in black and white: "Not included in this distribution permit are the books of Sacred Scripture."

"Sign here to indicate you understand the conditions and that you will not leave any of the Bible books in the village when you are there to distribute the other books," the official said, handing me a pen.

I shot up a quick prayer, "Lord, You know how to handle this problem; I don't. Please take over." And I signed on the dotted line.

A week later, a colleague and I drove to the Canela village in a pickup truck carrying a large metal drum packed solid with sixty sets of booklets in plastic bags. The Luke and Acts books were packed separately. The Canelas welcomed us with great joy since they had not seen us for over a year. We arrived in time for the late afternoon council meeting so the chief and the elders immediately ordered us to sit in the council ring and asked me to give a report. When they heard we had come to bring new booklets in their own language, they got excited and wanted me to show them the booklets. I opened a plastic bag of booklets and explained what was in each book.

When I finished, the chief noticed the plastic bag with the Luke and Acts books that I had not talked about. "What about those two thick books? Tell us what's in them!" he demanded.

No problem. I happily explained what was in the Luke and Acts books, at great length and detail, with frequent readings from some passages. When, after nearly an hour, I finished, they were more excited than before.

"Those are the best books of all," they exclaimed. "They tell us about Our Great Father in the Sky." I then showed them a copy of the document I had signed and explained that the government had forbidden me to leave any of the *God books* in the village.

The Canela leaders exploded in anger, "What? No way! Don't all the rest of the Brazilians have *God books* in their language?" they shouted, "Why can't we read them in our language? Don't we have the same rights as the Portuguese-speaking Brazilians!" They did. The Brazilian constitution clearly gives religious freedom to all its citizens.

They demanded I leave the books anyway. "Nobody will tell on you," they whispered. But I explained that as a guest in the country, I needed to obey the government's rules. Besides, I had promised, and I would not break my promise. Finally, the chief sent me to my house to sleep. "We'll figure something out in the morning," he said. We left to pray and sleep.

At dawn, the elders called me to their morning council meeting. "Here's what we've decided," they explained. "You pack all those booklets and the *God books* back into that drum. Put it on your pickup truck and leave the village. The chief's son will follow you on the village tractor. In thirty-five kilometres, you will go through the great gate. That is the end of the Canela Indian reservation. Your promise does not apply beyond the gate. Take the drum off your pickup and drive away. The chief's son will tie it securely to the back of the tractor. We already have a list with the names of the readers. When the chief's son returns, we will distribute the books to the readers. The *God books* as well as the reading booklets. That's our order. Do it!"

We did.

Years later, when we were able to resume our ministry in the village, we heard that the first books everyone had read were Luke and Acts, the special, forbidden *God books*.

The Canelas now read the published partial Bible. The front cover says, *Pahpam Jarkwa*, "God's Word." On the title page is *Pahpãm Jarkwa Cupahti Jõ Kàhhôc*, "The Book of the Highly Respected Words of God." In other words, "The *Holy* Bible."

⟡ COLUMN 42 ⟡
A CULTURE OF A THIRD KIND

My wife and I have been dealing with three strains of ATCK. No, it's not a new virus. It's our Adult Third Culture Kids: our three daughters, together for the Christmas holidays.

Valorie, Leanne, and Cheryl spent most of their formative years in Brazil, living both in the Portuguese-speaking Brazilian culture and the Canela-speaking indigenous culture. Every four years, they were exposed to Canadian culture for a year, and, after graduating from high school, studied in Canada, Germany, and the U.S.

They, like children of diplomats, foreign business people, missionaries, and those in the military, spent a good part of their growing-up years outside of their parents' home country, and they are comfortable in both their home and host countries, though they do not fully identify with either one. Third Culture Kids have a lot in common with each other, no matter what host country they lived in or what their "passport country" is. Throughout their lives they are a culture of their own.

Lucky for them!

Ruth E. Van Reken, co-author of *Third Culture Kids: the Experience of Growing Up Among Worlds*, describes the classic profile of a TCK as "someone with a global perspective who is socially adaptable and intellectually flexible."* Many immigrants have a similar profile. I was twelve years old when our family emigrated from the Netherlands to Canada. I lived in Canada for sixteen years before moving to Brazil to work as a linguist and Bible translator for twenty-four years. Although I am now back in Canada, I still travel at least four months per year in the U.S. I have often, like TCKs, wondered, "Who am I, really?" Some of us Third Culture Kids experience painful and difficult identity struggles. But, like many of them, I saw the variety

A CULTURE OF A THIRD KIND — 177

of experiences as gifts from God and learned to take the positive pieces and create a strong sense of, "This is *who* I am, no matter *where* I am."

Over twenty years ago, Dr. Ted Ward, a sociologist at Michigan State University, called TCKs "the prototype citizens of the future."** He foresaw what is increasingly happening in North America: children living within the context of multiple cultures becoming the norm rather than the exception.

U.S. President Barack Obama is a prominent example of an Adult Third Culture Kid, having lived much of his younger life in Indonesia and Hawaii. No wonder he invited other ATCKs to important posts in his administration: White House advisor, Valerie Jarrett (Iran and Great Britain); Treasury Secretary, Tim Geithner (East Africa, India, China, Thailand, Japan); National Security Advisor, James L. Jones (France); and Secretary of Commerce, Bill Richardson (Mexico).

Obama's colleagues on the Harvard Law Review noted both his exceptional skill at mediating among competing arguments and the aloofness that made his own views hard to discern—another typical feature of a Third Culture Kid. President Obama leans hard on his third culture strengths to deal with the world economic crisis, which requires some unconventional thinking and is the very thing TCKs are good at.

When God started to lead Jo and me towards ministry in Brazil, we often wondered how our daughters would adapt to the Brazilian and Canela cultures. We prayed much for them. Now we see the benefits: they are socially adaptable, intellectually flexible, have a wide global perspective, and are open to other worldviews. I am profoundly grateful. So are they.

No missionaries worth their salt would decide to get involved in foreign ministry "for the good of their kids." Yet it is comforting to know that when missionaries sacrifice the stability of home and the comfort of extended family and their own culture to do cross cultural ministry, God rewards them by making their children better able to cope in an ever-changing world.

This is probably a good place to put in a plug for getting involved in missions. Wycliffe's vision is to start a Bible translation program by the year 2025 in every one of the nearly 2,000 languages in the world that still need the Bible translated into them. All around the world, thousands of job positions are open in Wycliffe Bible Translators alone. Other mission agencies have similar needs.

Although some open job positions require applicants to take special training in linguistics and Bible translation, most job positions can be filled by people using the skills and abilities they already have—professions from accounting to zoo keeping (well, maybe not zoo keeping, but I needed a job that started with a Z).

By the way, here is what our three Adult Third Culture Kids have to say about their multi-cultural upbringing:

Valorie: "I'm glad I grew up exposed to such a wide variety of worldviews and cultures."

Cheryl: "I feel the positive benefits of my childhood in Brazil almost every day of my life."

Leanne: "I thank God that I am not like other people, small minded, bigoted, and inflexible in their attitudes . . . Juust kidding!!"

*David C. Pollock and Ruth E. Van Reken, *Third Culture Kids: The Experience of Growing Up Among Worlds* (Boston: Nicholas Brealy Publishing, 2001).

**http://www.tiu.edu/divinity/academics/faculty/ward

NEVER, NEVER RETIRE

Nearly fifty years ago, I stood in the pulpit of a church in central Alberta, as a brand new pastor, and preached my first sermon. I enjoyed telling God-stories as a young preacher then, and I enjoy telling them as an aged writer and speaker at banquets and conferences now. Since my wife and I have personally lived the God-stories I tell, I enjoy telling them even more than I did when we first started our life of ministry.

Ever since I entered my seventies, people have asked me, "When are you going to retire?" That simple question calls for a complicated answer.

I have already "retired" from many major jobs: from being a pastor after three years; from being a linguist, a literacy developer, and a Bible translator after twenty-four years; and from being an executive director of two Wycliffe organizations after nine years.

I used my storytelling skills in each of those major jobs, and though I changed jobs, I never retired from being a storyteller. More than a decade after retiring from the leadership positions, I still write weekly story-based columns. I still speak in churches and at retreats, conferences, and banquets, both in North America and overseas— about seventy events per year.

Nor have I retired from my primary "call" to grow more like Jesus every day. The apostle Paul compared his life to a race to attain the goal—to be just like Jesus. To grow up to be like Jesus is, of course, the goal to which each one of God's people is called. None of us can ever retire from that race!

I have a hard time understanding people who get a job they dislike and just hang in there until they can retire. God meant for us to use our abilities and enjoy our work. Ray Jenkins is a bit over-the-top, but he is my kind of man. He works a forty-hour week at his job as employee supervisor in Colchester, Vermont. He is past retirement age—way past—and in 2007, he was honoured at the Experience Works Prime Time Awards in Washington, D.C. as America's Oldest Worker for 2007—at 101 years old!

"When you retire, don't retire," Jenkins said. "Get another job, keep at it, keep on going. Keep your mind active. Keep your body going. You'll live."*

Barring complete physical or mental breakdown, I will never retire from using my God-given abilities to build His kingdom. Storytelling is one of those abilities, and no matter what position I hold or what organizational title I carry—if any—I will never retire from doing what I enjoy and can do well.

God did not create human beings to sit and do nothing. Without physical and mental exercise, our bodies and brains will atrophy. But we must be active doing things we enjoy. I used the word "enjoy" three times in the first paragraph for a reason. We cannot work for half a century at a job we hate without breaking down emotionally or physically.

When we stop moving from one job or interest to another, we are through with life. We need to keep changing our activities to keep ourselves alert. And not just our bodies—our minds too. What is the use of living a long life in a healthy body when our brain is off wandering about on its own?

I keep telling young people, "Find out what you like to do and what you are good at, and get training in it so you can do it even better. Get a job doing something you enjoy and can do well. You can quit a job, but you should never quit using your God-given strengths and abilities to build God's kingdom."

I also keep telling older folk, "When you retire from your job, don't retire. Get busy using your talents and abilities, the things you like to do. Use them to further God's work on earth, or use them in other circumstances, but *use* them. Never retire from using your abilities."

God does not mean for His people to sit in unending leisure, doing nothing to build His kingdom. He has plans for older Christians that go well beyond our youth and regular work.

Robert Browning said it well in the first stanza of his poem, "Rabbi Ben Ezra":

Grow old along with me!
The best is yet to be,
The last of life, for which the first was made:
Our times are in His hand
Who saith "A whole I planned,
Youth shows but half; trust God: see all, nor be afraid!"**

In my seventies, after five decades of focused work for God, I am well into "the last of life, for which the first was made."

Let the record show: It is definitely the good half!

---

*Emily Wood. "Experience Works Prime Time Awards 2007." Experience Works. 9 Oct. 2007 http://www.experienceworks.org/site/PageServer?pagename=News_Main#JenkinsNever ready to retire

**Browning, Robert. "Rabbi Ben Ezra." *The Oxford Book of English Mystical Verse*. Nicholson & Lee, eds. (Oxford: The Clarendon Press, 1917)

→ COLUMN 44 ←
THANK GOD FOR THE TROUBLEMAKERS

This New Year will be filled with major problems to solve and massive changes to cope with in many areas of our lives. National economies still struggle to recover from a worldwide economic recession. The Internet is alive with spam, scams, and malicious computer viruses that leave no one untouched. Around the world, terrorists continue to endanger or complicate the lives of even the most law-abiding citizens. Governments, businesses, and organizations are desperately looking for new, innovative ways to meet these and other major problems.

Here's some good news!

Every organization, from local church to national government has creative, innovative, problem solving people. Unfortunately, these folk are usually disguised as troublemakers, which is why administrators, pastors, and governments tend to ignore or expel them. This is not a good policy.

Sociologist Robert A. Heinlein (one of my favourite science-fiction authors), said it well, "A society that gets rid of all its troublemakers goes downhill."* So does a business, a church, or an organization.

Troublemakers are of two kinds: Those who need to be expelled, and those who need to be cultivated.

Some troublemakers care only for themselves and use the organization to give them what they want. Joshua 7 tells the story of the infamously selfish Achan. Joshua had given clear instructions that there was to be no plundering or looting. Achan disobeyed, and secretly kept some of Jericho's treasures for himself. As a result, some Israelites died in the next battle.

When Achan was discovered, Joshua said, "Why have you brought this trouble on us? The Lord will bring trouble on you today." Then they rightly stoned the troublemaker to death.

Other troublemakers are visionary, highly creative people, committed to the major goals of their organization, who see opportunities instead of problems. However, since their solutions are often highly creative and usually mean major changes for their organization, leaders see them as troublemakers and keep them at the outer fringes of the organization.

Jesus was such a troublemaker—an extreme case. The Jewish leadership disliked Him—He disturbed their comfortable lives. Jesus criticized everything from their rigid interpretation of God's laws, to their cozy arrangements with the Roman rulers who allowed them to rule the details of people's lives. From the periphery of distant Galilee, Jesus continually demonstrated His astonishing power to heal, to influence the crowds, and to show up the hypocritical selfishness of the ruling classes. Jesus showed up the leaders as He turned people towards God—the very job the leaders failed to do.

Instead of hailing Him as the promised Messiah, the leaders hauled Him off to execution.

Creative people still tend to cause trouble for leaders today. Businesses, churches, and societies are inclined to organize themselves to protect the most cherished, vital beliefs and ideas at the central cozy core—the board and leadership team. This structure, power, and institutional inertia all tend to inhibit innovative thinkers and drive them to the periphery where their innovative ideas are apt to stir up trouble.

The leadership at the centre is good at keeping things under control and preserving the status quo, but is often poor at innovation. Creativity happens naturally on the growing edge, which is by definition away from the centre.

A good leader knows how to identify troublemakers correctly. When he find those described in Proverbs 18:1, ". . . loners who care only for themselves and who spit on the common good" (*The Message*), the kind typified by Achan, the leader must isolate them. A good leader also seeks out the troublemakers on the fringe and carefully listens to them. Often they are innovative, creative thinkers who risk their own reputation and comfort to develop ideas and push for changes that could vastly improve the organization. A good leader cultivates these types of troublemakers.

Examples of breakthrough creativity on the outer edges abound. In the computer industry, for instance, phenomenal developments such as Apple and Google most emphatically did *not* start in the centre of an established company. They came from the outer fringes.

Where will leaders find the ideas that will save their organizations? Not usually among themselves or in their boardrooms, but among people out on the periphery. The implications for churches and Christian organizations are obvious. But there is a larger lesson as well.

Currently, the growing edge of world Christianity is not in the traditional centre—Western Europe and North America—but out on the edges.** South African Christianity developed the post-apartheid *Truth and Reconciliation* programs that saved the country. Korean churches have made massive early-morning prayer meetings legendary. Colombian citywide prayer meetings fill the largest city stadiums and impact the entire nation. The growth of Christianity in countries such as China where Christians are being inhibited and even persecuted can only be explained by the power of God. These things are not happening to any great extent in the centre of western Christianity. The creative growth is on the edges.

Where will the centre of Christianity find the ideas that will revive the Western and Northern Church? Not in Western Europe or in North America, but among God's people out on the periphery.

Christian leaders, teachers, and pastors need to listen carefully to nationals from countries outside of North America and Europe. They need to go to them—not to criticise, but to cultivate; not to teach, but to learn.

---

*"Robert A. Heinlein Quotes." Brainy Quote. 2010. http://www..brainyquote.com/quotes/authors/r/robert_a_heinlein.html

**Hanciles, Jehu J. "Migration and Mission: Some Implications for the Twenty-first Century Church." International Bulletin of Missionary Research (October 2003).

THE CASE FOR MISSIONS BEYOND THE LOCAL CHURCH

I visited my ninety-six-year-old mom recently and, as usual, enjoyed listening to her stories about her childhood. As I drove home, I thought of what the world was like in 1914, when Mom was born. Instead of the 6.8 billion people that currently live on earth, there were only 1.8 billion. Instead of the two billion Christians on earth today, there were only a few hundred million.

In 1914—nearly nineteen centuries after the Church received Jesus' commission to evangelize the world and make disciples of the nations—the job was not being done. "Why is world evangelization not complete?" Andrew Murray, pastor, and author of two hundred and forty Christian books asked himself a few years before Mom was born. His answer: "The vast majority of the Church has failed to take the job seriously. The denominations, groupings, and associations have focused the vision of their members, not on the need of the world, but on the need inside the congregation."*

Strong criticism, but well deserved. So, since then, has anything changed in the Church's attitude towards missions?

According to researchers for the Urbana 2000 missions conference, Murray's criticism was still valid.** They estimated that in the late 1990s the annual income of Christians around the world was US$12.3 trillion dollars. Of that amount, Christians gave only 1.7 percent to fund all Christian causes.

This means that out of every $1,000 earned, Christians gave only $17 to their church and other Christian work. Of that $17 given, $16 was spent in the local church and in home country ministries, leaving only $1 to be spent on foreign missions. Of that $1, only one cent funded work among the least evangelized: the hidden people groups.

In the year 2000, at least four billion people were still unreached by the gospel message. Although a large part of the Bible had been translated into nearly five hundred languages since Murray's criticism had been given, several thousand languages still had not had one word of the Bible translated into them.

That was the situation in the year 2000. What has changed since then?

While it is true that more young people go on short-term missions trips, and more retired people get involved in missions both at home and abroad, there has been little other positive change. The Barna Group conducts religious market research. None of their reports on the Church and missions in the past ten years indicate significant increases in giving or major improvement in reaching out beyond the local church.

On average, Christians, even in the more affluent countries, continue to give well below the biblical 10 percent. Poor stewardship and lack of prayer result in slow church growth in the home countries and continue to produce a severe lack of funding for overseas missions.

Mission agencies working overseas have highly qualified workers who are ready to train nationals, to teach needed skills, and to perform specialized tasks such as linguistic analysis. They are ready to go abroad, but they cannot take up their assignments simply because their local churches have not committed themselves to fully support them financially.

Trained nationals are ready to work in many areas of evangelism and church planting in areas such as Africa and Asia—which make up 72 percent of the world's population. Although the spiritual needs of these continents are enormous and opportunities abound, these gifted workers are hindered by a lack of funding.

Not only do we Christians give far below what God intends for us to give, but the little bit we do give is not being spent on fulfilling the Great Commission.

Of that measly $17, a full $16 is spent in the home church and in places such as North America which are already heavily evangelized. What's more, of the $1 that does go overseas, ninety-nine cents are used to fund work in people groups that already have some Christian population, while only one cent goes to fund work among the totally unevangelized.

Only one cent is given for the hidden people groups—the millions of people who speak languages in which the Bible has not yet been translated, the groups where there are no believers at all!

Out of every thousand dollars earned by Christians—just one little tiny penny—goes to fund evangelistic work among the most needy people groups of the world!

Is this God's financial plan?

No, I don't think so either.

God revealed His goal very clearly to the apostle John. Here is what John saw as recorded in Revelation 7:9-10:

After this I looked and there before me was a great multitude that no one could count, from *every nation, tribe, people and language*, standing before the throne and in front of the Lamb. They were wearing white robes and were holding palm branches in their hands. And they cried out in a loud voice: "Salvation belongs to our God, who sits on the throne, and to the Lamb" (NIV).

"From every nation, every tribe, every people and every language." That is inclusive.

After two thousand years of Christian history and twenty centuries of evangelizing and building churches, the Church may have reached every nation, but she has not yet reached every tribe or every people, and certainly not every language group with the Good News.

Nor will the Church succeed unless she makes some radical changes. Christians in all countries must start giving at a level that pleases God. Churches in every nation must staff and fully fund missions work among the most needy groups. Churches around the world must take on the responsibility to assure that every language in the world has at least some significant portion of the Bible translated into it.

When the whole world has been evangelized, when some from every nation, every tribe, every people, and every language group have chosen to repent and turn to God, then God's goal will have been met—the end result He has longed for will have been achieved.

Who knows? Maybe that is the moment God will say, "Son, it's time for the Second Going."

*Andrew Murray. *Key to the Missionary Problem*. (London: 1902)

**The Church Around the World; Lost People; Poverty, videos (Madison, WI: InterVarsity/ Urbana, 2000).

LET'S TAKE A BREAK FROM SYSTEMATIC THEOLOGY

"All Jesus did that day was tell stories—a long storytelling afternoon." This is how *The Message* puts Matthew 13:34, or as the KJV has it, "Without a parable spake He not unto them." This is a good description of what I do when I speak at conferences and on banquet tours. "All Jack did these past five weeks was tell stories—a long storytelling trip."

I am not the only storyteller who often travels about the country on Wycliffe sponsored tours. Five other teams, all equipped with storytellers, hold promotional Wycliffe Associate banquets in one hundred and fifty cities all over the United States each fall and spring on an eighteen-month cycle. Thousands of Christians from every kind of denomination, in four hundred and fifty cities are, therefore, learning missions theology—something few are exposed to in their home churches—and are learning it through stories, the way the crowds listening to Jesus did.

When Christians tell personal experience anecdotes of what God did in and through their lives, He adds a supernatural, Satan-defeating power to their stories (Rev. 12:11). Positive things happen to listeners of these power-infused missionary stories.

I tell the banquet guests how God used Jo and me to bring His Word to Brazil's Canela people in their own language. My talk is about thirty-five minutes long and is composed of fifteen short stories that show how God led the Canelas to accept us and how God met our needs. They also touch on language learning, literacy, Bible translation problems, the value of prayer, spiritual battles, and how God gave the ultimate—but costly—victory.

I do not try to preach or exhort, but, following the example of Jesus, just tell God stories.

People draw their own conclusions from these anecdotes, and many decide to get involved in Bible translation in their own way. Scores of individuals commit to intercede for missions more consistently than they had ever done before. Dozens indicate they want to get involved personally with a hands-on missions experience. Some give large one-time gifts, while others pledge to give monthly donations for a period of time. Other guests make a faith promise and launch out on a funding adventure with God, promising they will pass on certain amounts of money, on the condition that He brings the funds into their lives from outside their normal channels of income. All these responses just from hearing true stories!

It makes me wonder if we should take a break from the systematic theology we grew up with and develop a narrative theology. Our linear thinking North American/European culture loves to analyze, deconstruct, and dissect a piece of writing, believing that this is the best way to get to the truth. There is some value in this. But I doubt that it is what the first readers of the Bible did. They more likely just read the passages with open hearts and allowed the Holy Spirit to teach them whatever He wanted.

Canela culture is more like the ancient cultures of the Bible. The Canela elders let their stories carry their own message. They teach the young people their lore and tribal wisdom by telling stories of cultural heroes—how they lived, worked, planned, and strategized to fight and meet dangers together. When the elders tell traditional stories, they sing songs, they chant, and they jump up and mimic archers shooting enemies. They relive the action before their young audience, making the stories vivid and real.

What they would never do is analyze the story and pull out lessons to be learned. "Run every day," or "Practice shooting your bow and arrow." Instead, they simply allow their young hearers to draw their own conclusions from the stories.

My Bible has a hundred and sixty pages of New Testament narrative and only eighty pages of explanatory letters. Stories outnumber explanations two to one. Yet we Western Christians seem to focus on those eighty pages of explanation.

I wonder how many of our proudly held "denominational distinctives" are simply the result of our Western tendency to analyze each phrase in a Pauline epistle and formulate a new interpretation? When we see how denominational differences have torn the Body of Jesus apart, shouldn't we remember that Jesus prayed against this when He prayed "that all of them may be one" (John 17:21, NIV)?

How about just reading those stories and letters as the original, non-western readers did, taking them at face value, and allowing the Holy Spirit to apply their truths to our lives?

ALWAYS BE GENUINE—
EVEN IF YOU HAVE TO FAKE IT

"My Boss is a Jewish Carpenter," says the bumper sticker on the back of our mini-motor home. No Christian slogan or fish emblem, however, identifies our *car* as being operated by a Christian.

In our motor home, I never exceed the speed limit—even on the 110 km/h freeway I keep the speed to 90 km/h. It is the economics—the slower I drive the less wind resistance and therefore, less fuel consumption. On narrow roads, I happily pull over and let traffic behind me go past. Drivers smile and wave their thanks, and I feel like such a good Christian.

In our Chevy Tracker, it is a different story. I tend to drive it just a bit more aggressively. When it is safe to do so, I sometimes let the speedometer creep over the legal speed limit, do a *rolling stop* through some stop signs, and occasionally scoot through yellow lights. Hence, in my car, I would rather be anonymous.

Am I a hypocrite, or am I just being careful to "preserve a good testimony," as I was taught in the church I attended as a teenager? It is a small step from living a good, clean life, to hiding the not-so-good parts of my life so that people will think better of me than they would if they knew about the messy parts.

It is not easy being authentic all the time and in every circumstance. In Brazil, our German missionary friends followed their mission agency's policy against beer drinking during their four-year field term in Brazil, but when they returned to Germany for furlough, many of them drank beer with their prayer and financial partners.

Meanwhile, North American missionaries, working under a mission agency which had no rules against beer drinking, sometimes drank beer in their homes when they were in Brazil, but never touched a drop when they were on furlough among their archconservative supporting churches.

It reminds me of the slogan, "Always be genuine, even if you have to fake It."

Jesus spoke of greater and lesser commands (Matt. 23:23). For instance, He considered Sabbath keeping as one of the lesser commands and repeatedly demonstrated that healing the sick was more important than keeping Sabbath rules (Matt. 12:12).

Driving home from a church meeting in Rio de Janeiro well after midnight, I slowed as we approached a red traffic light. "Don't stop! Keep going!" a senior missionary shouted from the back seat. "If we stop in this neighbourhood, we'll be mugged!" I kept going. The greater law, "Avoid muggers!" trumped the legal, but lesser law, "Stop for red traffic lights."

We are rightfully appalled when we hear of some hypocritical church pastor exhorting his congregation to live a clean life sexually, while he himself visits prostitutes and is addicted to pornography.

What should bother us even more, however, is how our North American Christian churches tend to fixate on certain commands, mostly having to do with sex and related issues such as abortion and same-sex marriage, while ignoring global issues that are vastly greater.

A church so badly governed that the pastor can keep his position for years while committing immorality is horrible. What is far worse, however, is tens of thousands of Christian churches that are so badly taught and so poorly motivated that they ignore the huge global problems in the world around them.

Millions of North American Christians watch the news on television and see extreme poverty, rampant disease, insidious illiteracy, constant wars, corrupt leadership, and distressed environment, all exacerbated by a pervading spiritual emptiness. How many of us ask ourselves, "What should the Christian church do about these horrible problems? What should our local church do? What should I and my family do?"

The Bible is packed with commands to God's people to build His Kingdom and to deal with these major global problems in His way.

At the core of God's government is faith, which of course, comes through His Word translated into the languages spoken by every person on earth.

As followers of Jesus, we believe that, but we must be careful to make sure that what we strongly *believe* matches what we *say* and that both match what we *do*. I suspect some of us Christians sitting in church are just going through the motions. We bow our bodies in prayer, but our minds are not involved and our hearts not engaged.

Some of us stand and sing loudly and passionately about our total commitment to God and His Kingdom, but ten minutes later, when the offering plate comes around, we drop in a tip—not a tithe—and have no intention of ever helping a local ministry, going on a missions trip, or doing our part to solve a global problem.

We have Bibles in our homes and carry one to church. It all looks good, but how many of us consistently read significant amounts of God's Word every day, asking Him to connect what we read with what we see on TV?

Driving home at 1:30 in the morning on a deserted country road, we come to a stop sign at an intersection. Do we really need to come to a total and complete stop? Probably.

God, however, is vastly more concerned with our need to pray intensively, to give generously of our finances and ourselves, and to soak our minds and emotions in His Word. Then, after we close His Book, He wants us to love Him, to act in love towards others, and thus build His Kingdom. Anything less is faking it.

THE DAY I BLEW IT AS A SPEAKER

I was seventeen when my pastor asked me to give a ten-minute devotional at the following week's Sunday night service. The subject was "faith," and it would be the first time I had "preached" publicly.

I had no problem with that. A few years before, I had begun to live life as a Christian and had attended that church for about a year. I liked telling stories to friends. I had a larger than normal size ego and, thus, no fear of standing up in front of a crowd. I figured I would do pretty well in my talk. After all, faith is a common Christian concept, and it should be easy to talk about.

It did not work out that way.

That Sunday night, I confidently got up to speak, excited but not scared, and started talking. "Faith is important," I told the congregation, but I did not say *why* it was. I told them that everyone should have faith, and more of it, but I did not say *how* a person could get more faith. I quoted no Scripture, told no illustrative stories, made no comparisons, and presented no arguments. All I did was repeat a number of platitudes about faith and then repeated them again. Finally, after four minutes of empty rhetoric, I said, "So let's all have more faith." I sat down, knowing I had failed, and failed miserably, but not knowing exactly why.

I felt like a carpenter full of excitement and confidence building a shed using rotten scrap lumber and bent rusty nails, working without a tape measure and using a stone as a hammer. The result was obviously awful.

Instead of a hero, I was a zero. My self-esteem hit bottom. But that is not always a bad place to be. It was from there that I turned to God, to whom I should have turned in the first place. I prayed, "God,

I messed up. I don't know why. Now what? Where do I go from here, if anywhere?"

A few years later, I started studying at Bible school and learned what was missing from my talk. I discovered that ego and scraps of general knowledge were not enough to produce a speech that God could use to bless my hearers. It needed some content. Out with the empty clichés; in with relevant biblical passages. Out with the platitudes; in with inspiring stories. Out with the time-filling repetitions; in with practical application.

Applying what I had learned, I spoke frequently at young people's groups, in rescue missions, even on street corners—far more often than my peers did. I should have felt good, but I didn't. I still felt like a failure. Although I filled my speeches with solid content, pertinent Scripture, and inspiring stories, and my hearers seemed to enjoy listening to me, nothing much seemed to be happening to them. Where was the impact? Where were the results?

I still felt like a carpenter. One who, having built a good-looking shed with proper tools and superior materials, is astonished to see the whole thing tumble down—nails slithering out of lumber as if the law of friction had been repealed, leaving the law of gravity to take over.

My speaking was still worthless, and I told God so.

That is when I remembered the passage in the Psalm 127:1 "Unless the LORD builds the house, its builders labour in vain" (NIV). Hmm, and I suppose the same applies to public speakers. Unless the Lord builds the speech and talks to the hearers, the speaker talks in vain. As that truth soaked into my mind and heart, my speeches and their results began to change.

Eventually, over decades of experience and input from scores of people, I learned to pray specifically for three areas when preparing and making a speech, presentation, or sermon:

Pray first for the topic: "Father God, what have You given me, what experiences have You led me through, and what are You saying to me about what these people need to hear?

Pray for the content: "Master Jesus, what have You said about this topic in your Word? You told stories; what stories can I tell to focus people's attention? You used metaphors; what comparisons can I use to help people understand? What are some practical things that I can suggest they could do about this topic?"

Pray for the result: "Holy Spirit, unless these people hear Your voice speaking in their hearts, all I am doing is entertaining them. Please help them make decisions about what You are telling them. Help them to obey You, and act on what You are saying."

I pray these prayers constantly when I am preparing for a public speaking event, whether it is an informal five-minute talk or an intensive, major multi-session weekend ministry, and God does answer my prayers. Sometimes I see results immediately—people coming to me to ask in-depth questions about a career in missions, some making major financial commitments, others picking up literature, buying books, promising to pray. At other times, I hear of results months, even years, later.

I still have a healthy ego, and I am still excited, not fearful, about speaking in public, but after fifty-five years of learning, I think I am finally getting the hang of it.

I need God's help to prepare as well as I can. I need His help to remind me of appropriate stories. And I need to remember that the final result is totally in His hands.

And that takes faith. "So let's all have more of it!"

INVESTORS WHO MISS OUT

David Cowan made a heartbreaking mistake. As a venture capitalist with Bessemer Venture Partners, his job is to invest in potentially successful companies and increase the value of their stock. One day a friend told him about two young Stanford students who were building an Internet search engine and needed money to launch their company. David refused to meet with them, and the students found their start up money elsewhere, naming their new company, Google. Because of David's mistake, Bessemer's investors lost the chance to make billions of dollars over the next decade.*

It was not the first time Bessemer missed out on opportunities to make profitable investments. Apple Computer offered shares that valued their company at $60 million. Bessemer thought it was outrageously expensive and did not invest. Apple is now worth more than $145 billion. Bessemer also sent eBay away empty handed and turned down the company that would become Compaq. They refused to invest in FedEx seven separate times. Bessemer and its client investors repeatedly lost the opportunity to make billions of dollars because they failed to invest in companies that became highly profitable to their stockholders.

It breaks my heart when I see investors missing out on enormously profitable opportunities.

The investors I am concerned about are not David Cowan and the Bessemer company. My focus on the millions of men and women all across North America who have money to invest in ways that will bring a good return to the One who gave them the money—the Ultimate Owner. Churches are full of these money managers, and for the most part, they are missing out on great opportunities to invest—investments that would benefit millions on earth and fatten the investors' bank accounts in heaven.

As Christians, we are God's money managers, and most of us are doing a terrible job. According to surveys by The Barna Group, the average Christian church-goer invests less than 3 percent of their income in God's work.** Those who do give, Barna reports, give mostly as consumers—paying for the church building program, the church programs, and church staff salary—all of which benefit the givers directly. Relatively little money goes to fund cross-cultural missions that focus on meeting the physical, educational, and spiritual needs of people who otherwise have no hope.

Barna also reports that only 9 percent of North American Christians give at least 10 percent of their income to God's work, either through their local church, or through other ministries. Why do so few Christians give less than 10 percent? Is it because they think tithing is a Jewish law given by Moses, something like the command to keep a *kosher* diet? They need to be taught that giving 10 percent of our income to God's work as an act of worship did not start with Moses. It was Abraham, who today's believers emulate as the *father of faith*, who practiced tithing many hundreds of years before the concept was codified in the law of Moses.

God, through Moses, commanded the Jewish people to tithe. It is debatable whether Christians are under the same strict compulsion to tithe. There is no doubt, however, that God wants His people to give, and give generously and in proportion to how He has prospered us. Ten percent is an excellent guide to proportional giving. We need to think of the tithe as the beginner, entry level of investment—the floor, not the ceiling.

Unfortunately millions of North American Christians are holding onto money that desperately needs to be invested in God's work. That is why every missionary working in cutting edge, cross-cultural, pioneer missions can tell you stories of people, programs and ministries that suffered from lack of funding—not because there is no money in the hands of God's money managers. No, God has supplied abundantly. He has done His part. It's because His managers are not investing as they should.

Just this week, I heard of yet another missionary family—one with seven years of experience and a MA in a Bible translation academic discipline—who had to leave the field and their mission agency mostly because of lack of investors. Someday the investors who failed to partner with them financially are going to be chagrined when they see how they missed out.

God has done at least three things to help people invest money to build His Kingdom:

He has set a vision before us and authorized us with a commission to evangelize the world and disciple the nations (Matt. 28:18-20).

As the Source of all wealth, He continually supplies all the money we need to accomplish that task (Phil. 4:19).

He has set up a faith-based motivating system to encourage us to invest. Every time we give to further God's work on earth in ways that do *not* directly benefit us personally, God credits that amount to our heavenly bank account (Luke 14:13-14; 18:22).

Church leaders sometimes see para-church agencies as competition—always looking for church people to staff and money to fund their para-church ministries. I am convinced that if local churches were spiritually revived, competition would turn into cooperation, tipping would turn into tithing, and vital ministries of every kind would be flooded with volunteers and awash in money.

Investors would be delighted. So would God.

*Steve Maich. "Unleashing the Power of Screwups." *Maclean's* 121.18, May 2008: 29.

**"Americans Donate Billions to Charity, but Giving to Church Has Declined." The Barna Group, April 25, 2005.

⊹ COLUMN 50 ⊹
LIVING THE
EIGHTY-ONE PERCENT LIFE

What is a Christian? Ask that question in North America, and you might well get hundreds of contradictory answers. Some respondents would use terms such as wild-eyed fanatic, anti-abortionist, anti-gay extremist, and religious nut. Others would describe a Christian as a believer in God, a caring and generous person, and a responsible citizen. The rest would be somewhere in between those two extremes.

Among the Canela people of Brazil, however, there is no confusion. A Christian is a *Jeju kôt ipa catê*—a "Jesus-after-walk-person" or "Jesus follower." The Canelas simply take the term used for Jesus' disciples in their translation of the Gospels and apply it to themselves when they begin to follow His teachings.

The term "Christian" originally meant exactly that—a "follower of Jesus Christ." But now, the term is confusing and ambiguous, making me wish we could replace it universally with the much clearer "Jesus-follower."

After all, a follower, or disciple, is exactly what Jesus calls His people to be. A student wants to know what his teacher *knows*. A disciple wants more than that. An apprentice wants to learn to do what his master *does*. A disciple wants more than that. A disciple wants to become what his teacher or master *is*. That is why we, as Jesus-followers, focus our whole lives on becoming just like Jesus.

He should be our focus, but often He is not. Instead, we focus on beliefs and doctrines, or on side issues of every sort, all the while forgetting we are supposed to simply become more like Jesus.

Ray Vander Laan,* in his lecture, *In the Dust of the Rabbi*, said, "An internationally known Orthodox Jewish rabbi once said, 'Any Christian who tells me he is a disciple of the Rabbi *Yeshua* (Jesus) and who does not read the four Gospels at least once a month is a liar. How are you going to know your Rabbi if you don't spend time reading what He did and what he said?'"

When I heard that quote, I started reading three or four chapters of Matthew, Mark, Luke, and John per day. Not that I didn't know what was in them! I have read the Gospels at least once a year for the past fifty years, and of course, translated them verse by verse into Canela. Even so, I surprised myself by how much I was learning about Jesus that did not match what I experienced and was taught in church.

I was taught to be separate from the world, yet Jesus was known as "a friend of sinners" (Matt. 11:9).

I was taught to preach conversion, yet Jesus preached the Kingdom of God, with justice for all, and mentioned conversion simply as the entrance requirement (Matt. 6:33, John 3:5).

I see and hear of Christian leaders exercising power and demanding to be served, yet Jesus came to serve, not be served (Matt. 20:28). I see and hear of Christians who love to fight for their opinions, who split churches over minor differences in interpretations, who are abrasive, confrontational, and divisive. Yet Jesus brought people together. He was a peacemaker and reconciler. He broke down the traditional barriers between genders, races, and social strata.

The Christian Church seems to focus on the beginning and the ending of Jesus' life. Christmas and Easter are two huge celebrations in the Church and in the culture.

We celebrate Christmas with a special holy day, with pageants, concerts, gift giving, and all sorts of cultural hoopla. The Gospel writers, however, devoted only 8 percent of their writings to describing Jesus' birth and first thirty years of life.

The same is true for Passion Week and Easter Sunday. The Church celebrates these events with passion plays, music, and liturgies. Yet the Gospel writers allocated only 11 percent of their writings to describe Jesus' arrest, death, resurrection, and ascension.

All the rest, 81 percent of the Gospels, describe what Jesus said and did—what He taught and demonstrated. The Gospel writers, under the guidance and inspiration of God's Holy Spirit, described at length how He lived and how He interacted with other people. In four out of five pages, they focused on His teachings, His conversations, His confrontations, His miracles, and His travels. They wrote so we could obey His teaching and imitate His life, not just celebrate His birth, death, and resurrection.

I once heard of a large church that uses a refreshingly different procedure for preparing and approving new members. Instead of indoctrinating the prospective members with all their denomination's distinct beliefs and practices, they simply ask a potential member to tell the congregation how she became a Jesus-follower. After that, any member of the church is free to ask her any question relating to the way she lives her life. The only catch is that every question has to be based on Jesus' Sermon on the Mount—Jesus' summary on how we should live.

That church, like the Canelas of Brazil, wants its members to be true Jesus-followers. Thus, they emphasize and focus on Jesus and His teaching.

Makes sense. After all, you tend to hit what you aim at.

*Ray Vander Laan, "In the Dust of the Rabbi" http://www.zondervan.com/Cultures/en-US/Product/ProductDetail.htm?ProdID=com.zondervan.9780310271192&QueryStringSite=Zondervan

THE LANGUAGE OF CHRISTMAS

So there I was, standing with the rest of the congregation and entering into the spirit of Christmas, when in the middle of singing a carol, I got a rude shock—an unpleasant linguistic surprise.

"Angels we have heard on high, sweetly singing o'er the plains . . ." So far so good.

As I sang, I visualized the scene: flocks of sheep asleep under the starry night sky; the watching shepherds by their little campfire in the Judean hills; the sudden appearance of the angel of God with his announcement of the birth of the long-awaited Messiah; and, of course, the blast of light and music as the heavenly choirs burst onto the scene with their song of praise and promise.

But then my vivid mental picture was shattered when we started singing the chorus, echoing what the angels sang, *"Gloria in excelsis Deo!"*

What?! What nonsense is this?! Latin? What were those angel choirs thinking? Why on earth would they sing in Latin, the language of the hated Roman oppressors? The language of the occupying soldiers!

No, those Christmas angel choirs didn't sing in Latin. Of course not. They sang in the native language of the shepherds, in Aramaic—the language the shepherds' forefathers had learned to speak centuries before, during several generations of exile in Babylon.

Singing about the greatness of God to Judean shepherds in Latin would make as much sense as singing to North Americans in the Canela language. I can hear it already, *"Quê ha côjkwa kam mehcunea jirôpê, Pahpãm pejti ne cati na me harẽ!"*

What an uplifting blessing! . . . Not!

God, the Great Linguist, always communicates to people in their own language. In the beginning, he spoke directly to Abraham, Moses, and the prophets in Hebrew, the language of the people of Israel. That is why almost the entire Old Testament was written in Hebrew.

Later on, through His Son Jesus, God spoke Aramaic to the Jewish people in Palestine. For many years, the stories about Jesus and His teachings circulated as oral traditions in Aramaic.

In the meantime, the most important, most used language in the Mediterranean region was Greek, and through translation, God spoke Greek to millions of people. Several generations before Jesus was born, scholars translated the Old Testament from Hebrew into Greek. Matthew, Mark, Luke, and John eventually translated the stories about Jesus, His teachings, and parables from Aramaic into Greek and wrote them down. The rest of the books of the New Testament were also written in Greek.

Several hundred years later, through the work of Jerome the Bible translator, God communicated in Latin to millions of people in Europe and the Mediterranean region who spoke Latin as their first language. By the way, the Bible was not translated into the high classic forms of either Greek or Latin used by scholars and the elite, but into ordinary Greek and Latin—the language spoken by people in their homes and on the streets.

All this flashed through my mind as I continued singing that Christmas carol. We sat down, and during the announcements, I scribbled some notes for this column. I also jotted a reminder to look up the comments Dr. Lamin Sanneh, a professor at Yale Divinity School and converted Muslim, had made during a lecture* some years before.

Among world religions, Christianity is unique in many ways: Christianity is the only world religion that has no special "Holy Language." Hebrew is not, nor is Greek. Neither Latin nor English are "Holy Languages," not even the English of King James' time. To God there are no unclean cultures or improper languages. In one sense, every language and every culture can, through Bible translation, become a "Holy Language."

Christianity is the only world religion in which almost none of the actual words of the Founder are preserved in the language in which He spoke them. Jesus spoke Aramaic, and except for a half a dozen phrases such as His words from the cross, every word from His mouth we know only from the Greek translation.

Christianity is the only world religion that spreads through translation of the Bible, its foundational document, into other languages. Right from the beginning, Christianity was a translated religion, the only world religion that is propagated almost totally outside the language of the Founder.

Christianity is the only world religion that adopts the indigenous names for the High God, the God of the Bible: El, Yahweh, Theos, Deo, Deus, Gott, God, Pahpam, Tupan, Imana, Yala, Kalunga, and thousands more.

Christianity is the only world religion that has no cultural or geographical centre. Christianity is as much at home in a cave in Cambodia as in a cathedral in Canberra.

Christianity is the only world religion whose Holy Book is, by far, the most translated book in the world. It has been translated in whole or in part, or is being translated right now, in nearly five thousand languages. Bible translation project are expected to be started in the remaining two thousand languages of the world by the year 2025.

Christianity is also unique in that it flourishes where the Bible is read in the ordinary, mundane, everyday language of the people. On the other hand, Christianity is weak and anaemic where believers are forced to read a Bible that is not in their own heart language. The very reason God revealed Himself in the Bible is so He would be known by people in every language and ethnic group. The Bible, therefore, exists to spread Christianity.

By abandoning Jesus' mother tongue, Christianity has liberated the Good News to every language. No language is incapable of fully holding the truth. No language is the only one in which the truth is fully encapsulated.

So is there a language of Christmas? Yes. *Any* language is the language of Christmas when the full meaning of Christmas is transmitted to the mind and heart of the hearer or reader.

As God, through Luke, says in Canela, "May those in the sky shout how surpassingly great and good Our Father is. And may those on earth, towards whom Our Father causes good to come, experience a deep down peace in their innermost being."

This Christmas may you shout God's praise and experience His deep down peace.

*Wycliffe International Conference. Jaars Centre, Waxhaw, NC. May 30, 1996.

ALL THAT IS AROMATIC
IS NOT COFFEE

It is the week between Christmas and New Year's—time to relax with family, reminisce, nibble turkey leftovers, and drink coffee. Hmm, about coffee . . .

My mother was the first to lie to me about coffee: "If you drink coffee when you are small, you will grow up having red hair." As a little Dutch boy, I could think of nothing worse than having red hair. So I limited myself to enjoying the smell of the coffee that my parents, uncles, and aunts drank in copious quantities and wishing that I would grow up quickly so I could drink coffee like them.

Now that I have grown up, I drink coffee whenever I can, which, because I travel a lot, is not as often as you might think. Many clean-living, generous, and seemingly honest men and women have invited me to enjoy a good cup of coffee. The enticing smell forces me to accept with alacrity, only to find that they lied to me. What smelled like good coffee in the mug was not. It could perhaps, most charitably, be called a "coffee flavoured hot drink."

Captain Kathryn Janeway, commander of Star Trek Voyager, said, "Coffee, the finest organic suspension ever devised." She was right—just as she was when she rescued Seven-of-Nine from the Borg.

Good coffee is distinguished by three qualities:

1. Body—that lingering pleasant taste after you swallow. Brazilian coffee is justly famous for body.

2. Acidity—the liveliness or energy found especially in the fruity aroma and savour of East African coffees.

3. Roast—light, medium and dark, to fit the type of coffee bean used.* For example, Jamaican Blue Mountain coffee, which James Bond called "the most delicious in the world" tastes best as a dark roast.**

Coffee, however, has long suffered from a bad reputation. Generations of doctors have warned against it. Some religious groups forbid the drinking of coffee, putting it on the same level as life–destroying, intoxicating drinks or addicting narcotics. They warn that the caffeine in coffee often causes jitteriness and sometimes leads to violent outbursts of anger. That is probably true for some people, just as eating peanut butter will kill those allergic to it. My philosophy is, "There is no such thing as coffee that is too strong, only coffee drinkers who are too weak."

I realize that some people dislike coffee, but I always wonder, "Have they ever tasted *real* coffee?" Or did they base their dislike on having experienced the bitter dregs of some over-boiled, reheated, old slop, or some namby-pamby weak swill? I introduced my grandkids at a very young age to proper coffee. *Grandpa's Candy Coffee* is what they gleefully call the small cups of well-sugared espresso.

Coffee's bad public image was finally corrected by a study published in the June 2008 issue of the prestigious *Annals of Internal Medicine*. Research scientists at the *Autonomous University of Madrid* and the *Harvard School of Public Health* tracked 129,000 people for over twenty years.***

They concluded that, compared with those who shunned coffee, men who drank five cups of coffee a day were 44 percent less likely, and women 34 percent less likely, to die of heart disease. What's more, coffee drinkers were less likely to die prematurely from any cause— men 35 percent less and women 26 percent less.

And that's not all. Drinking coffee lessens the likelihood and severity of diseases such as Alzheimer's, many types of cancer, liver disease, Type II diabetes, depression, gallstones, kidney stones, and Parkinson's. (And, Mom, no researchers reported any coffee drinking children growing red hair!)

The disproved lies about coffee make me think of the continuing lies about God and Christianity. A couple of books that were published a few years ago, *The God Delusion* and *God is Not Great*, restate the same old, tired opinions and lies about God.

I realize some people dislike Christianity, but I always wonder: have they ever tasted *real* Christianity? Or did they base their dislike on having experienced the bitter dregs of some over-boiled, reheated, old, opinionated Christianity, or some namby-pamby, weak religion with no convictions of any kind?

Have they ever met a group of people who are actually disciples of Jesus? People who display the true reality of Christianity in the same way I present true *Candy Coffee* to my grandkids?

Christianity's bad public image will be corrected some day. Not by a study based on a few hundred thousand people, but by all the multi-billions of people who have ever lived on earth falling as one to their knees before Jesus Christ confessing, "You are the Master of all!" (Phil. 2:11, *The Message*).

In the meantime, it is up to us to recreate the first Christmas when Jesus took on a human body. We must let Jesus live His life through us and, like coffee, exhibit Christian *body*—that lingering good taste that is undeniably like Jesus. We need to show some *acidity*— that aromatic liveliness and energy as we live out the resurrected life of Jesus. And, like the *aroma* of freshly made coffee, we need to smell like Jesus. "Thanks be to God, who . . . through us spreads everywhere the fragrance of the knowledge of him. For we are to God the aroma of Christ among those who are being saved and those who are perishing" (2 Cor. 2:14-15, NIV).

As followers of Jesus, we must be willing to undergo a process of suffering, analogous to being roasted, so these qualities will emerge to their fullest.

Body: the lingering taste. Acidity: the unique aroma. Roast: the proper heat to bring the other out. For coffee or for Christians, all three are needed.

*Theodore Erski. "Cupping Around the World—Bean There, Drunk That." *Sky Delta: A Traveling Magazine* November 2008: 39-42.

**Live and Let Die. Directed by Guy Hamilton. 1973. United Artists.

***Robert Ebish. "It's Official: Coffee is Good for You." *Sky Delta: A Traveling Magazine* November 2008: 66.

STUFF: LEAVING A LEGACY

For many decades, the most published book in the world was the Bible. Notice the tense. It *was*. But it no longer *is*.

In 2001, far more copies of another book were annually published and distributed. No, it is not Chairman Mao's Little Red Book. That is a distant third after the Bible. Although 100 million Bibles are printed and sold or given away each year, this new book has increasingly surpassed the Bible in its number of printed copies that are distributed annually.

What is this new book? It is nothing other than the IKEA catalogue! Yes, the famous household furnishing catalogue! In 2001—over 100 million, in 2003—115 million, in 2006—160 million, and in this last year, 198 million copies of the IKEA catalogue were published!

We live in a world that is obsessed with getting things and then more things. The popularity of the IKEA catalogue is only one example. The Mall of America in Minnesota, with 520 stores dedicated to distributing things, measures 4.2 million square feet (390,192 square metres), and is large enough to house thirty-two giant Boeing 747 planes. It attracts more visitors annually than Disney World, Graceland, and the Grand Canyon combined.

But that's nothing in comparison to the West Edmonton Mall, which is just a half hour's drive from where Jo and I live. WEM, with its 6 million square feet (557,418 square metres), has 800 stores and services, employs 23,000 people, and receives 150,000 visitors a day. Oh, and there are plans to expand too.

What is it with all the material goods that seem to sneak into our homes, basements, and garages? How do we attract so much stuff? I honestly thought Jo and I were different. I thought we knew how to control the influx of things. When we first left for Brazil, everything we owned fitted in a few duffel bags and half a dozen boxes. Twenty-five years later, we sold or gave away household items, tools, and books to the extent that the five of us arrived in Canada with only a dozen boxes, suitcases, and duffel bags. But now, as we face an impending move into town, we have discovered that in the past two decades, stuff seems to have seeped back into our lives, filling every nook and cranny, every closet and cupboard, and every shelf and storage bin.

It reminds me of the Bible story where the ancient Israelites unsuccessfully searched for Saul to make him king. God Himself had to tell them where he was. "Behold, He hath hidden himself among the stuff." Saul could easily hide himself in our garage, and no one but the Lord could find him! I hate having this much stuff!

What has changed? What now drives me to ruthlessly get rid of, give away, throw out, cut back, and scale down the number of our physical goods? It is the fear that I might spend the last decade of my life simply being the custodian of stuff accumulated during my lifetime. I do *not* want to fill the rest of my life packing my old things, moving them, and taking care of them. I want to get *new* stuff! No, no. I'm just kidding.

I want to free up time that is now consumed with sorting and searching for what I want among all the stuff I do not need. I want time to organize a legacy to leave my children and grandchildren. Jo and I have large boxes of videos and photos. We have keepsakes from our children's early lives; we have memories, and we have stories. I have a suitcase full of handwritten diaries and many megabytes of journals, prayers, and Popjes personal history on my computer.

These are the types of things I wish I had more of from my grandparents, from my parents, and from my aunts and uncles. These are the physical things I want to pass on in a useable, accessible format to my family.

Jo and I, like all the rest of us, hope that we have already passed on many intangible and less physical, but far more important things to our family. We agree with the concept that contentment does not come from having all our wants supplied—it comes from reducing our wants to include only the essentials of life, like food, clothing, and shelter, so that we can focus on getting more of righteousness, godliness, faith, love, patience, and meekness (1 Tim. 6).

Those essential intangibles are a legacy far more important than a few thousand dollars inheritance and a house full of stuff. At least Jo and I hope so. We also want to leave a great collection of family stories, organized photos, and a few keepsakes—small ones.

One of those small keepsakes would be a publication. No, not the IKEA catalogue or Mao's Red Book, but that red Canela Bible. That alone is a major legacy. Jo and I thank God every day that He used us to bring His Word to the Canela people for the first time. So do many of our prayer partners and financial supporters. They too can age happily, knowing they have helped to leave a legacy that will continue on long after they are dead and buried.

A legacy they will enjoy even in eternity.

---

*Breen Pierce, Linda. *Simplicity Lessons: A 12-Step Guide to Living Simply.* Carmel: Gallagher Press, 2003.

About Jack Popjes

Jack was born in the Netherlands and immigrated to Canada in 1950 with his family. He attended Berean Bible College in Calgary. Jack and Jo were married in 1962 and pastored a Baptist church in Innisfail, Alberta, for three years before joining Wycliffe in 1965. They left for Brazil in 1966 with three pre-school daughters and began work with the Canela people in 1968.

When the Popjeses began work with the Canelas, the villagers were illiterate, and there were no believers. By the time the Scriptures in the Canela language were dedicated in 1990, there were many Canela believers, all able to read the Bible and teaching others to read and obey the Word.

After the Popjeses left Brazil in 1990, they served Wycliffe Canada as regional representatives. While serving as a rep, Jack honed his skills as a public speaker at numerous conferences and hundreds of promotional banquets.

Jack was appointed by the board as the director of Wycliffe Canada in 1994 with a mandate to lead the organization through a large number of changes.

After two three-year terms as director of Wycliffe Canada, Jack was appointed director of Wycliffe Caribbean and asked to strengthen the organization and to recruit and train a successor. He completed this task in May 2004.

Currently Jack is Wycliffe Canada's national representative, serving as a speaker and writer. He speaks at about sixty-five events per year in Canada, the U.S., and overseas. He writes a weekly column called "The Look," which goes out to over one thousand subscribers around the world. He has published two books, *A Poke in the Ribs,* and *A Kick in the Pants,* which are collections of his best columns.

CONTACT

You may contact the author utilizing the following methods:

Email: jack_popjes@wycliffe.ca

Paper mail: Box 85, Suite 1, RR 1, Onoway, AB, T0E 1V0 Canada

To receive the weekly *Look* column via email, send a blank email to Look-on@lists.wycliffe.org

Check the author's website (www.thewordman.ca) for archived articles, speaking calendar and more information.

To order additional copies of this book contact the Wycliffe Media Resource Center by calling 1-800-WYCLIFFE or email mrco@wycliffe.org to place your order.

To order an autographed copy of this book, contact the author directly.